Smart Alec's

SPOOKY JOKES

I DON'T BELIEVE IN GHOSTS

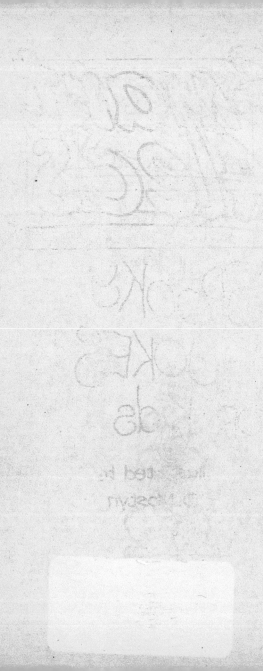

Smart Alec's

Spooky Jokes for Kids

Illustrated by
D. Mostyn

BEAVER
PUBLISHING

© World International Publishing Limited 1988

First published in Great Britain in 1987
by Ward Lock Limited. This edition published
in Great Britain by Beaver Publishing Limited,
Alderley Edge, Cheshire SK9 7DT

Typeset by Columns of Reading
Printed and bound in Finland by UPC Oy

British Library Cataloguing in Publication Data

Smart Alec´s spooky jokes for kids.
  I. Alec, *Smart*
  828´.91402   PZ8.7

  ISBN 1-85962-007-8

  This edition 1997

What kind of spook can you hold on the tip of your finger?
  A bogey!

Did the bionic monster have a brother?
  No, but he had a lot of trans-sisters.

1st Undertaker: I've just been given the sack.
2nd Undertaker: Why?
1st Undertaker: I buried someone in the wrong grave.
2nd Undertaker: That was a grave mistake.

Spook: Should you eat spiders and slugs and zombie slime on an empty stomach?
Witch: No, you should eat them on a plate.

GHOSTLY UGH!

FLICK THIS CORNER OF YOUR BOOK
THROUGH FROM THE BACK AND SEE
SMART ALEC OUTSMARTED BY BLACKIE
THE MONSTER. IT'S HAUNTING!

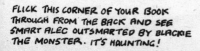

Did you hear about the phantom who ate the Christmas tree decorations? He died of tinselitis.

How do you get a ghost to lie perfectly flat?
   You use a spirit level.

Did you hear about Sid the spook? He got drunk so often he was known as the methylated spirit.

What's Count Dracula's favourite breakfast?
   Readyneck.

A hairdresser, a carpenter and a lollipop lady were out for a ramble in the forest one day when they got lost. Night fell and they all became alarmed as they stumbled through the trees, not knowing where they were going. At last, in a clearing, they spotted a little shack, its lights glowing an eerie blue colour in the moonlight. 'Shelter!' cried the hairdresser. 'Let's go in,' said the carpenter. 'It looks a bit creepy to me,' warned the lollipop lady. 'You two go in first.' So in went the hairdresser — and came face to face with an ugly old witch.

'What do you do for a living?' she asked.

'I'm a hairdresser,' he said. And so she took a pair of scissors and cut off all his toes.

The next one in was the carpenter. 'What do you do for a living?' the witch asked. 'I'm a carpenter,' he replied. And so she took out a saw and sawed all his toes off, one by one.

Finally the lollipop lady, who had been listening all the time, came in very nervously. 'I'm a lollipop lady,' she said very defiantly. 'So you'd better suck all *my* toes off!'

Woman in bed: Aaagh! Aaaagh! A ghost just floated into my room!
Ghost: Don't worry, madam, I'm just passing through.

On which side does a monster have most of its fur?
　　The outside.

1st Witch: Two of my pet spiders just got married.
2nd Witch: Really?
1st Witch: Yes – it's so nice to have newly-webs around.

Who got higher marks in the History exam – Smart Alec or the prehistoric monster?
　　The prehistoric monster. He passed with extinction.

Did you hear about the horrible hairy monster who did farmyard impressions? He didn't do the noises, he just made the smells.

What do you call a witch who drives very badly?
　　A road hag.

What was Dr Jekyll's favourite game?
　　Hyde and Seek.

There once was a ghost from Darjeeling
Who got on a train bound for Ealing
It said at the door
'Please don't sit on the floor'
So he floated up and sat on the ceiling.

*What's the difference between Beethoven and a
dead body?*
   One composes and the other decomposes.

How does Dracula keep fit?
   He plays batminton.

*'Waiter, waiter,' called a diner at the Monster
Café. 'There's a hand in my soup.'*
   'That's not your soup, sir, that's your finger
   bowl.'

Where do undertakers go when they retire?
  Gravesend.

What do you get if you cross a ghost, a helpful boy and a vegetable?
  An invisible Brussels sprout.

1st Monster: My boyfriend says I have cheeks like peaches and ears like petals.
2nd Monster: Yes, football 'peaches' and bicycle 'pedals'.

If a flying saucer is an aircraft, does that make a flying broomstick a witchcraft?

Dr Frankenstein: We won't be cold this winter! I've just crossed a sheep with a porcupine.
Igor: And what did you get?
Dr Frankenstein: An animal that knits its own sweaters.

What did Tarzan say when he saw the monsters coming?
    Here come the monsters.
And what did he say when he saw the monsters coming with sunglasses on?
    Nothing – he didn't recognize them.

How can you tell if a vampire has a glass eye?
    It usually comes out in conversation.

A monster who came from Devizes
Had noses of different sizes.
One was so small
It was no use at all –
But the other won several prizes.

What do you get if you cross a ghost with a packet of crisps?
   Snacks that go crunch in the night.

Why did the werewolf cross the road?
   Because the chicken was on holiday.

What's white, built on sleek lines, and beats other spooks from a standing start?
   A turbo-charged phantom.

A flute player was walking home late one night from a concert. He took a short cut through the local woods, and he hadn't gone far before he bumped into a ghost and then a vampire. Pulling out his flute he began to play a lovely trilling melody – and the ghost and the vampire stood entranced. Soon the musician was surrounded by a crowd of phantoms and monsters and goblins and cannibals and witches listening to the music. Then up bounded a werewolf. 'Yum! Yum!' he growled, and he gobbled up the flute player.
   'Why did you do that?' complained the others. 'We were enjoying it.'
   'Eh, what was that?' said the werewolf.

What do mermaids eat for breakfast?
  Mermalade.

1st Witch: What's your black cat's name?
2nd Witch: Dunno, he won't tell me.

*What do you call a monster with gravy, meat
and potatoes on his head?*
  Stew.

Why is it so difficult to become a coroner?
  You have to take stiff exams.

The villagers of Lower Bumpstead were going on a Midsummer picnic, but unfortunately they forgot to invite the elderly lady who was believed by some to be a witch. On the morning of the picnic the vicar suddenly realized what had happened and went to invite her to come along.

'No thanks,' said the old lady. 'I've already cast my spells, and I don't want to get soaked or attacked by a swarm of bees.'

Dracula: Have you seen the new monster from Poland?
Frankenstein: A Pole?
Dracula: Yes – you can tell him by his wooden expression.

1st Witch: Beer cans, old newspapers, lolly sticks, orange juice cartons . . .
2nd Witch: Shut up, you're talking rubbish again.

Why did Dr Frankenstein have his telephone cut off?
   Because he wanted to win the Nobel prize.

Why does Count Dracula sleep in a coffin?
   Because the council won't give him a flat.

What do phantom football supporters sing?
   Here we ghost, here we ghost, here we ghost!

Did you hear about the monster with one eye
at the back of his head and one at the front?
He was terribly moody because he couldn't
see eye to eye with himself.

Lady Jane Grey
Had nothing to say.
What could she have said
After losing her head?

Who wrote Count Dracula's life story?
  The ghost writer.

What did his friends call Yorrick at school?
  Numbskull.

Rumours that Count Dracula is about to
marry Glenda the Ghoul are not true. They're
just good fiends, that's all.

What should you give short elves?
  Elf-raising flour.

Do werewolves always snore?
  Only when they're asleep.

What do Egyptian monsters put on their toenails?
  Nile varnish.

Where does Dracula keep his savings?
  In the blood bank.

Why are werewolves such good comedians?
  They make people howl with laughter.

How do you know when there's a monster hiding under your bed?
  When you wake up your nose is squashed against the ceiling.

Old Ghost: I'm going to give up haunting.
Young Ghost: Why?
Old Ghost: I don't seem to frighten people any more. I might as well be alive for all they care.

Two little boys went scrumping for apples one evening and were chased by the owner of the orchard. They ran into a graveyard just as it was getting dark and hid behind a gravestone. One of the boys dropped his apples and two of them rolled over towards the gate. 'We'll pick them up on the way out,' he said. 'While we're waiting for it to get really dark, let's divide the apples between us.'

It just so happened that an old lady was taking a short cut across the graveyard that night, and as she passed the gravestone she heard a little voice saying, 'That's one for you and one for me, one for you and one for me . . .' In terror she ran to the gate and into the arms of a passing gentleman.

'Help!' she cried. 'There are ghosts in the graveyard and they're dividing up the bodies!' Nervously they stepped back into the cemetary. And through the darkness came a whispering voice, 'There's one for you and one for me. Oh, and don't forget those two over by the gate . . .'

Ghost: How do you do?
Spook: How do you do what?

What did the boy monster squid say to the girl monster squid?
   'I want to hold your hand, your hand, your hand . . .'

Why are old ghosts boring?
   Because they're groan-ups.

Vampire: You know, they say blood is thicker than water!
Victim: So what? So is porridge!

What is the best-selling cannibal book?
  'How to Serve Your Fellow Man'

Monster Mum: Did you put the cat out?
Little Monster: Was it on fire again?

Why did the wooden monsters stand in a circle?
  They were having a board meeting.

Dr Frankenstein decided to build an extension to his laboratory, so he crossed a cement mixer, a ghoul and a chicken. Now he's got a demon bricklayer.

What did the angry monster do when he got his gas-bill?

He exploded.

A boy monster and a girl monster were out on their first date. Despite being very shy, things seemed to be going well, and they went for a drive in the boy monster's lorry. Suddenly he stopped. 'Shall I show you where I had my operation?' he asked.

'All right,' stammered the girl monster.

'Right,' said the boy monster starting the lorry, 'it's second left at the traffic lights and straight down the high street.'

1st Monster: Where do fleas go in winter?
Werewolf: Search me!

1st Witch: I like your toad. He always has such a nice expression on his face.
2nd Witch: Yes, he is nice. It's because he's a hoptimist.

I'M NOT A TOAD! I'M A FROGGIE.

Where does the Sandman keep his sleeping sand?

In his knapsack.

A monster walked into a shop selling dress fabrics and said, 'I'd like 6 metres of pink satan for my wife.'

'It's *satin*, sir, not satan,' said the assistant. 'Satan is something that looks like the devil.'

'Oh,' said the monster, 'you know my wife?'

Frankenstein: Help, I've got a short circuit!
Igor: Don't worry, I'll lengthen it.

What did the smelly monster say when the wind changed?

It's all coming back to me now.

Smart Alec: Our school is haunted!
Silly Billy: Really?
Smart Alec: Yes, the head teacher's always talking about the school spirit.

What is a skeleton?
   Someone who went on a diet and forgot to say 'when'.

Ugly Monster: I got 150 Valentine cards last year.
Witch: That's amazing!
Ugly Monster: Yes, it is. The only problem was that I couldn't afford to post them all.

Where do monster stingrays come from?
   Stingapore.

A big monster went to the pictures and sat in front of a little boy. 'Can you see?' asked the monster.

'No I can't,' said the boy.

'Well,' said the monster. 'Just watch me and laugh when I do.'

How can you tell when you're in bed with Count Dracula?

He has a big D on his pyjamas.

Smart Alec: Do you know that there's a monster in disguise hiding up every oak tree?
Silly Billy: That's ridiculous.
Smart Alec: Have you ever seen one?
Silly Billy: Certainly not.
Smart Alec: That just shows how well it works!

Have you heard about the mad monster comedian?

He kept trying to joke people to death.

1st Witch: Why are you using a goldfish to cast your spells?
2nd Witch: I can't afford a black cat.

Did you hear about the Irish monster who built a wooden car? Wooden seats, wooden engine, wooden wheels. The only problem was, it wooden go.

What's grey and hairy and can see just as well from either end?
A werewolf with its eyes closed.

Monsters are so romantic. Did you hear about the one who bought his wife a fur coat for her birthday?
He gave her two steel traps and a shotgun.

What was written on the bionic monster's gravestone?
    Rust in peace.

What do you call a short vampire?
    A pain in the knee.

What are the posh giant's favourite pastimes?
    Haunting, shooting and fishing.

Why did the monster buy a sledgehammer?
    To burst his spots.

1st Monster: I've been working so hard at terrorising people I feel half dead!
2nd Monster: Shall I arrange for you to be buried up to your waist?

1st Ghost: Who's that walking down the street?
2nd Ghost: The invisible man.
1st Ghost: He looks like a real wally.
2st Ghost: Don't be rotten – can't you see he's not all there?

Where do Red Indian ghosts live?
   In creepy tepees.

How did the witch's frog die?
   It Kermitted suicide.

Werewolf: The Bride of Frankenstein has a lovely face.
Ghost: Only if you read between the lines.

Seen in the local newspaper:
THE ANNUAL MEETING OF THE
CLAIRVOYANTS CIRCLE HAS HAD TO
BE CANCELLED DUE TO UNFORESEEN
CIRCUMSTANCES.

*What did the monster say when he saw Smart
Alec asleep in bed?*
   'Yum yum! Breakfast in bed . . .'

*What comes out at night and goes 'Munch,
munch, ouch!'*
   A vampire with a rotten tooth.

A short, fat, hairy monster was waiting for a
train and decided to while away the time by
weighing himself on a machine on the station
platform. Once he'd weighed himself he
looked at the chart that indicated the ideal
weight for each height.
   'Having any problems?' asked another
passenger. 'Are you overweight?'
   'No,' said the monster, 'I'm just four feet
too short.'

What should you do if a ghost comes in through the front door?
  Run out through the back door.

Dracula: Why did Igor lose his job?
Monster: Illness.
Dracula: Anything serious?
Monster: Dr Frankenstein got sick of him.

Did you hear about the absent-minded monster who went round and round in a revolving door for three hours?
He didn't know if he was coming or going.

If you're a regular at the Monster Café you'll know that it isn't famous for either the quality or flavour of its food. Only the other day a vampire called the waiter over.
  'Is this coffee or tea?' he asked. 'It's disgusting – it tastes like disinfectant.'
  'In that case it's tea,' said the waiter. 'Our coffee tastes like paraffin.'

Ghost Postman: Is this letter for you? The name's smudged.
Ghost: No, my name's George Ghastly.

Witch: I'm going crazy!
Monster: Why?
Witch: The werewolves next door have just had a baby, and it howls all night.

Phantom: You know, there are some kinds of monster which have never been seen.
Spook: Yes, like yetis.
Phantom: Hasn't anybody seen one?
Spook: Not yeti.

How does a ghost count to ten?
  One, boo, three, four, five, six, seven, hate, nine, frighten!

Are Igor and Dr Frankenstein much fun at parties?
  Yes, they keep everyone in stitches.

Mother Vampire: The shame! How can I face the neighbours?

Monster: What's happened?

Mother Vampire: A zombie just tripped over in the playground and my boy Vince fainted at the sight of blood!

Why do ghosts like living in tall buildings?
  Because they have lots of scarecases.

Smart Alec: If you don't believe in ghosts I dare you to spend a night in the haunted house.

Silly Billy: No, I *don't* believe in ghosts, but I might be wrong.

Why do monsters find it difficult to swallow vicars?
  Because you can't keep a good man down.

Zombie: Where does your Mum come from?
Abominable Snowman: Alaska.
Zombie: Don't worry, I'll ask her myself.

What kind of cake do monsters hate most?
  Cakes of soap.

Did you hear about the vampire comedian?
He swalled an Oxo cube and made a laughing stock of himself.

Why did the monster have his sundial floodlit?
  So that he could tell the time at night.

What's black and bounces?
  A rubber witch.

Mrs Monster: My son drank a tin of lighter fuel yesterday.
Mrs Ghost: What happened?
Mrs Monster: He ran up and down the stairs fifty times, flew around the front room, raced into the kitchen and went bang slap into the washing machine.
Mrs Ghost: Was he dead?
Mrs Monster: No, he just ran out of petrol.

Two monsters were brought up in court for fighting in the street. 'It was self-defence,' said the pink monster. 'The blue monster bit half my ear off.'
  The magistrate wasn't impressed. 'You are bound over to keep the peace for a year,' he thundered to the blue monster.
  'Oh, your honour, I can't do that,' he cried. 'I threw it away.'

Spook: What does coincidence mean?
Phantom: Funny, I was just going to ask you that.

Why did the monster eat yeast and shoe polish?
 He wanted to rise and shine.

Monster: Doctor, I swallowed a clock last night.
Dr Frankenstein: This could be serious – why didn't you come to see me earlier?
Monster: I didn't want to cause any alarm.

What did the headless coachman say when the green giant asked to borrow some money?
 Sorry, I'm a bit short.

A monster who lived in Penzance
Ate a small boy and two of his aunts.
A cat and a calf,
A pig and a half –
And now he can't button his pants.

What did the three monsters play in the back of the Mini Metro?
   Squash.

1st Cannibal: I'm going to become a vegetarian.
2nd Cannibal: Why?
1st Cannibal: You can go off people, you know.

Mrs Monster: Did you hear what happened to my son?
Mrs Spook: No – what?
Mrs Monster: He fell into a liquidizer.
Mrs Spook: Oh dear, he always was a crazy mixed-up kid.

Werewolf: Werewolves are smarter than ghosts, you know.
Ghost: I never knew that.
Werewolf: See what I mean?

What's the best way of warding off ghostly doctors?
   Always carry an apple with you.

Witch: I've never been so insulted in my life! I went to a Hallowe'en party and at midnight they asked me to take my mask off.
Spook: Why are you so angry?
Witch: I wasn't wearing a mask.

Did you hear about the monster who ate little bits of metal every night?
It was his staple diet.

Smart Alec: Yesterday I took my girlfriend to see *Maggie the Monster's Revenge*.
Silly Billy: What was she like?
Smart Alec: Oh, 8 feet tall with two heads, green hair, a bolt through her necks . . .
Silly Billy: I meant your *girlfriend* . . .

What do you call a monster moth with a wingspan of 20 feet?
   A mam-moth.

What did the shy pebble monster say?
   I wish I was a little boulder.

Why did the turb-charged robot get stiff joints?
   He had vroomatism.

Who did the vampire marry?
  The girl necks door.

Why did the bald monster hang out of windows?
  To get some fresh 'air.

What's pink and grey and wrinkly and old and belongs to Grandpa monster?
  Grandmother monster.

Frankenstein's Monster: Did you like the dictionary I gave you for Christmas?
Dracula: Yes – I simply can't find words to thank you.

Once upon a time there was a bald ghost-hunter who went to stay for the night in the Haunted House. After dinner he went up to the Creepy Bedroom, where a terrifying ghost had been reported. He changed into his pyjamas, brushed his teeth, climbed into bed and then took off the wig he always wore and hung it on the bedpost. Then he settled down for a really spooky night. But by midnight the ghost still hadn't materialized and he dropped off to sleep.

'Some haunted house,' he grumbled when he woke up the following morning. 'I haven't slept so well for years.' He reached out automatically for his wig on the bedpost and was just about to put it on without thinking when he noticed something extremely odd – the wig had turned snowy white . . .

Why do undertakers go to the Earl's Court Exhibition Centre each year?
For the Hearse of the Year Show.

Why did the little monster do so well in his exams?
  Because three heads are better than one.

What do short-sighted phantoms wear?
  Spooktacles.

Why should you always be calm and polite when you meet cannibals?
  There's no point in getting into a stew, is there?

Dr Frankenstein: How are fangs, Dracula?
Dracula: Not too good – I'm 50 litres overdrawn at the blood bank.

Heavenly Father, bless us,
And keep us all alive.
There's three of us for dinner –
We'll be cooked at half-past five. .

Do ghosts like going horseriding?
  Yes, they're very fond of ghoulloping.

How much did the psychiatrist charge
Frankenstein's monster for his first visit?
  £20 for consultation
  £50 to repair the doorway
  £200 for a new couch

What do you call a phantom with a frankfurter
on its head?
  A head banger.

On what day of the week do monsters eat
people?
  Chewsdays.

Who won the monster beauty contest?
  No one.

1st Monster: I went to the circus last night.
2nd Monster: So did I. What did you think of the knife-throwing act?
1st Monster: I thought it was boring. He threw twenty knives at that soppy girl and missed every time.

Did you hear about the phantom who was engaged to a monster? When she found that he had a wooden leg – she broke it off, of course.

Define a very loud noise.
   A skeleton dancing on a roof.

A little monster came home from school in tears. 'What's wrong?' asked his mother.
   'It's the children at school,' he sobbed. 'They keep calling me big head.'
   'Don't take any notice of them,' said his mother. 'They're only jealous. Would you go and do some shopping for me? We need five pounds of potatoes, two pounds of sugar, six apples, six oranges, two loaves and a dozen eggs.'
   'All right,' said the little monster. 'But where is the shopping basket?'
   'The handles are broken, dear, but don't worry. Just use your school cap instead.'

Smart Alec: I wish I had enough money to buy a huge monster.
Silly Billy: Why do you want a monster?
Smart Alec: I don't – I just want that much money.

Did you hear about the two monster frogs who went into a restaurant together? One of them ordered lunch but the other just sat silently. Eventually the other frog turned to him and said, 'What's wrong? Don't you want any lunch?'

'I'm sorry,' whispered the frog, 'but I've got a man in my throat.'

Why did the undertaker chop all his corpses into little bits?
    Because he liked them to rest in pieces.

Did you hear about the short-sighted monster who fell in love with a piano?
It had such wonderful white teeth, how could he resist it?

Skeleton: I'm never going to a party again.
Monster: Why, what happened?
Skeleton: I went to one last night and people kept hanging their coats on me.

1st Monster: Every time we meet, you remind me of a famous film star.
2nd Monster: Meryl Streep? Madonna? Raquel Welch?
1st Monster: No, E.T.

Why did Nelson's ghost wear a three-cornered hat?
   To keep his three-cornered head warm.

Smart Alec: Did you hear about the big blue monster who took first prize at Crufts?
Silly Billy: How could a monster get a prize at Crufts?
Smart Alec: He ate it.

AA-A-A-ARREST T-T-T-THAT SP-SP-SP-SPOOK

George worked for many years as a waiter, until one day he died. His wife was quite overcome with grief and decided to try to get in touch with him through spiritualists, mediums, fortune-tellers, anyone she could find – but none of it worked.

Then one day a friend came to visit her, and when she heard about the problem she had an idea. 'I think it's quite possible that if George was haunting anywhere, he'd be haunting the restaurant where he used to work,' she suggested, 'Why don't you go there and try again?' The wife followed this advice and went to the restaurant, where she sat at a table and called for her husband to contact her.

'George, it's me,' she cried. 'Are you there?'

'Yes, I am,' whispered a ghostly voice.

'Speak louder, I can't hear you,' begged his wife.

'I can't,' came the ghostly whisper.

'Then come over to this table.'

'I can't do that,' said George's ghost. 'It's not my table.'

Did you hear about the bike that was possessed by devils and went around biting people?

It was known as the vicious cycle.

Witch: How does it feel to hurtle through doors and walls?
Ghost: It hurtles.

1st Witch: Where's your toad?
2nd Witch: He's out doing some spying for me.
1st Witch: Spying?
2nd Witch: Didn't you know? He's a croak and dagger agent.

How do monsters count to thirteen?
  On their fingers.
How do they count to forty-seven?
  They take off their socks and count their toes.

Igor: There's a ghost here to see you, sir.
Dr Frankenstein: Tell him I can't see him.

There once was an old witch called Rose,
Who had several huge warts on her nose.
So she had them removed:
Her appearance improved –
But her glasses dropped down to her toes.

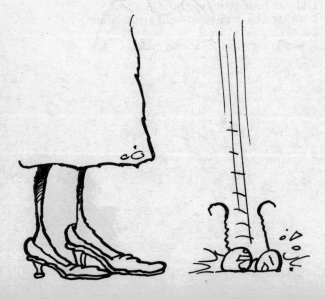

Did you hear about the little spook who couldn't sleep at night because his brother kept telling him human stories?

Which ghost was president of France?
   Charles de Ghoul.

1st Ghost: Did you read in the paper about the two tribes of cannibals who went to war against each other?
2nd Ghost: Terrible, wasn't it? Apparently the winners made mincemeat of the losers.

Why did the monster eat a lightbulb?
   Because he was in need of light refreshment.

How do cannibals like their shepherd's pie made?
   With real shepherds. *

* SEE
'SMART ALEC'S
REVOLTING JOKES
FOR KIDS'.

HEY! WHAT'S THIS JOKE DOING IN THIS BOOK!

A monster raced into the doctor's surgery. 'Help me, doctor,' he cried, holding a handkerchief to the back of his neck.

'What's wrong?' cried the doctor.

'I hit the back of my neck,' said the monster.

'How did you do that?'

'I stood on a table.'

What's the difference between a deer which is being chased and a short witch?

One's a hunted stag and the other's a stunted hag.

Little Ghoul: I want to join the Boy Scouts.
Mother Ghoul: Why?
Little Ghoul: I want to learn to tie knots for nooses.

Did you hear about Dr Frankenstein's friend the plastic surgeon?
He sat on a radiator and melted.

Mummy, mummy, come quick! There's a monster in the toilet.
What's it doing?
Drinking all the water!

Did you hear about the Yorkshire lady who dressed all in white so that she would be seen by traffic on dark winter nights?
She scared fourteen people to death before she was knocked down by a snowplough.

Witch: I've just invented this potion. Want to try it?
Ghoul: What is it?
Witch: You take one sip and you tell the truth.
Ghoul: Okay, pass the bucket. Slurp . . . Yuck! It's paraffin!
Witch: And that's the truth!

Knock, knock.
Who's there?
Bet.
Bet who?
Bet you never thought you'd be eaten by a monster!

1st Witch: Did you have any luck with your advert for a husband?
2nd Witch: I got seven replies. They all said, 'You can have mine!'

Why did the Egyptian ghost worry?
  Because her mummy was a daddy.

Why did the werewolf go to the barber?
  He couldn't stand his hair any longer.

The Reverend Postlethwaite was a very
famous missionary. He gave the cannibal
tribesmen of Upper Oomperland their first
taste of Christianity.

The wizard who'd invented a flying carpet was
interviewed for the local radio station. 'What's
it like, Merlin, to fly on a magic carpet?'
asked the radio interviewer.
  'Rugged,' replied Merlin.

Algy met a bear.
The bear met Algy.
The bear was bulgy.
The bulge was Algy.

Monster: I've just had the bolts removed from my neck.
Ghoul: Have a scar?
Monster: No thanks, I don't smoke.

Some cowboys were sitting around a campfire late one night telling each other stories. 'I know a Red Indian who never, ever forgets anything. The Devil can have my soul if I'm lying,' boasted one.

That night the Devil, who'd been listening, appeared to the cowboy and said, 'I warn you, if you were telling a lie about that Red Indian I'll take your soul when you die.'

'I'm not,' said the cowboy. 'Come and meet him yourself.'

The two of them went to where the Indian had pitched his tepee and the Devil asked him one question. 'Do you like eggs?'

'Yes,' said the Indian. This was enough for the Devil, and he and the cowboy went off on their own separate ways. Some years later the cowboy died and the Devil collected his ghost and took it back to the Red Indian to see whether he remembered them.

'How!' said the Devil, greeting the Indian in the traditional way.

'Scrambled,' replied the Indian.

What single word describes the spooky sight of 100 cakes doing the tango?
  Abundance.

1st Spook: I hear you've got a new job.
2nd Spook: Yes, I've started working for a spiritualist.
1st Spook: Is he much good?
2nd Spook: Oh, medium, I'd say.

How do you know if there's a monster in your custard?
  When it's *really* lumpy.

1st Cannibal: I don't think very much of your chef.
2nd Cannibal: Just eat the vegetables then.

Igor: Dr Frankenstein's just invented a new kind of glue.
Dracula: I hope it doesn't make him stuck up.

Three travellers were crossing the bleak moors one night when a terrible storm blew up. Soaked to the skin and freezing, they made their way towards a dim light that flickered in the distance. When they reached it they discovered an eerie-looking house, with tall, twisted chimneys and hideous gargoyles leering down at them from the eaves. Despite their fears they knocked and the door was opened by an old crone wearing long black robes and with horrible warts all over her face.

'Come in, my dears,' she smiled, revealing that most of her teeth were missing. 'I had a feeling that you were coming.'

Nervously the travellers entered the hall, which was full of purring black cats. A bat hung upside down from the lightbulb. 'Can you put us up for the night,' stammered one of the men.

'Oh yes,' said the witch. 'But before I show you up to your beds, would you like a hot drink? Hot chocolate or coffee?'

'Hot chocolate for me, please,' said the first man.

'Coffee for me, please,' said the second man.

'I'll have hot chocolate,' said the third.

Which just goes to show that two out of three people prefer hot chocolate before they go to bed at night.

The vampire went into the Monster Café.
'Shark and chips,' he ordered.
'And make it snappy.'

1st Monster: What's that horrible green thing on your shoulders?
2nd Monster: Aaaagh! Get it off!
1st Monster: Don't panic, it's your head.

A huge hairy monster went to the doctor to ask for help because he was becoming very weak. The doctor prescribed some pills and a tonic to build him up. A few days later the monster came back to the surgery.
'Are you feeling stronger?' asked the doctor.
'No,' said the monster. 'The medicine isn't working – you see, I can't get the tops off the bottles.'

Why are most monsters covered in wrinkles?
Have you ever tried to iron a monster?

1st Monster: Have you seen my new dog? He's got no legs and I call him Cigarette.
2nd Monster: Why Cigarette?
1st Monster: I have to take him outside for a drag.

IF I WASN'T SO BUSY RUNNING AWAY FROM THE GHOST - I'D BITE THAT JOKE!

In a dim, dark lane there was a dim, dark
  house,
And in that dim, dark house there was a dim,
  dark attic,
And in that dim, dark attic there was a dim,
  dark oak chest,
And in that dim, dark oak chest there was a
  dim, dark suitcase,
And in that dim, dark suitcase there was a
  GHOST!

Where was Dracula when the lights went out?
  In the dark.

Monster: Stick 'em down!
Ghost: Don't you mean stick 'em up?
Monster: No wonder I'm not making much
money in this business.

Dr Frankenstein: With Christmas coming up,
Igor, I'm going to try a seasonal experiment
and cross an octopus with a chicken.
Igor: Why?
Dr Frankenstein: So that everyone can have a
leg for dinner.

Boris the monster knocked on a witch's door
and asked for something to eat. 'You look
familiar,' said the witch. 'Didn't I give you
some bat's blood soup last week?'
  'Yes,' said the monster, 'but I'm better
now.'

There was an old lady who had earned herself a wonderful local reputation as a weather forecaster – in fact she was so accurate that many people thought she was a witch. People came from far and wide to see her before they booked their holidays or sowed their crops. But one day there was a lot of concern because the old lady stopped making her forecasts. An old farmer, who'd always relied on her predictions, went to see her. 'Please,' he begged, 'tell me the best day to sow my wheat. You've always got the weather right before.'

'I can't,' said the old lady.

'Why?' asked the farmer. 'Have your special powers deserted you?'

'No,' said the old lady. 'My radio's broken.'

Why do monsters wear glasses?
  So that they don't bump in to other monsters.

1st Ghost: My son's so stupid!
2nd Ghost: Why, what does he do?
1st Ghost: He keeps climbing walls.

Knock, knock.
Who's there?
Frank.
Frank who?
Frankenstein. **✳**

✳ SEE 'SMART ALEC'S KNOCK-KNOCK JOKES FOR KIDS'
YOU'LL BE KNOCKED OUT!

CLEVER JOKE
BY ME – STARVING
ARTIST

Father monster came home from the Monster Repair Company to find his son Boris in disgrace. 'He's been fighting again,' said mother monster. 'It's those terrible Slime children down the road. They're such a bad influence on him. He learned all about punching and kicking from them.'

'Yes,' interrupted Boris, 'but hitting them on the head with an axe was my own idea.'

1st Witch: I'm going to cast a spell and make myself beautiful. I'll have hundreds of men at my feet.
2nd Witch: Yes, chiropodists.

The wonderful Wizard of Oz
Retired from business becoz
What with up-to-date science
To most of his clients
He wasn't the wiz that he woz.

What do vicars write in?
  Exorcise books.

What jewels do monsters wear?
  Tombstones.

1st Cannibal: Am I too late for lunch?
2nd Cannibal: Yes, everyone's been eaten.

Why does Frankenstein's monster go click-click-click-click?
  It's just his bones knitting.

What's the difference between a lemon and a purple monster?
  A lemon is yellow.

Why did the stupid monster give up boxing?
  He didn't want to spoil his looks.

Hickory, dickory, dock,
The monster ran up the clock.
The clock is now being repaired.

It was late one night and a cyclist on the way back home had a puncture. He propped his bike up against the cemetery wall and examined the tyre, but there was nothing he could do about it – he was going to have to walk home. And the shortest route was through the cemetery. It was very dark and very creepy as he opened the gates and went in. Lightning flashed across the sky and in the distance he heard the church clock strike midnight. Suddenly he heard a strange tapping sound coming from one part of the cemetery and, despite his nervousness, he went over to see what was happening. He peered out from behind a gravestone and saw a shadowy figure all in white and holding a hammer and chisel.

'What are you doing?' asked the man nervously.

'Just correcting my headstone,' said the thing in white. 'You see, when they buried me they spelled my name wrong . . .'

Why does Count Dracula give lessons in bloodsucking to young vampires?
  He likes to bring new blood into the business.

How can you spot a monster on Come Dancing?
   He's the one with three left feet.

Where do ghosts go for holidays abroad?
   The Ghosta Brava.

1st Ghost: I don't agree with you at all!
2nd Ghost: Why not?
1st Ghost: There's absolutely no evidence that people exist.

Why did the one-eyed monster give up teaching?
   What's the point with only one pupil?

There once was a doctor who lived in the house next door to one of his most awkward patients. The patient made a real nuisance of himself. If he didn't feel well during the day he'd run into the back garden and yell over the garden wall, 'Doctor, doctor, can you give me something for my tummy ache?' And if he didn't feel well in the night he'd bang on the wall, no matter what time it was, and shout, 'Doctor, doctor, can you give me something for my cold?'

Finally, after many years, the patient died. The doctor's relief didn't last long because a few days later he too died, and by an amazing coincidence they were buried side by side in the graveyard. It was quiet and still in the cemetery, and the church clock struck midnight. Suddenly the doctor heard a ghostly banging on the side of his cold, dark coffin, and a spooky voice said, 'Doctor, doctor, can you give me something for worms?'

1st Cannibal: I don't like my wife.
2nd Cannibal: Yes, you're right. A bit more pepper and some garlic would help, I think.

Why did the lady monster wear curlers at night?
    She wanted to wake up curly in the
    morning.

*What did Tarzan say when the werewolf
chewed his leg off?*
Ah-eaaah-eaaah!

Little Monster: Mummy, mummy, I don't
want to go to Australia!
Mummy Monster: Just shut up and keep
swimming.

Ghost: I've been invited to an avoidance.
Monster: An avoidance? What's that?
Ghost: It's a dance for people who hate each
other.

A cannibal chief was just about to stew his
latest victim for dinner when the man
protested, 'You can't eat me – I'm a
manager!'
    'Well,' said the cannibal, 'Soon you'll be a
manager in chief.'

Did you hear about the stupid werewolf? It lay down to chew a bone and when it got up it only had three legs.

Mrs Monster: I'd like a dress to match my eyes, please.
Shop Assistant: I don't think we've got any bloodshot yellow dresses, madam.

A salesman walked up to the front door of a house, rang the bell and, when the door opened, sprinkled dust along the path and into the hall.

'What's this?' asked the surprised housewife.

'It's ghost dust,' explained the salesman. 'You just sprinkle it on the ground and you don't suffer from ghosts.'

'But we don't have ghosts anyway,' protested the housewife.

The salesman just smiled. 'You see, it works!'

What is even more invisible than the invisible ghost?
His shadow.

Smart Alec: Something terrible just happened to the jelly monster.'
Silly Billy: What?
Smart Alec: It set.

1st Witch: I bought one of those new paper cauldrons they've been advertising on the TV.
2nd Witch: What's it like?
1st Witch: Tearable.

Why is the letter T so important to the sticky monster?
   Because without it he'd be the sicky monster.

A monster walked into a music shop and asked the owner for a mouth organ. 'This is extraordinary,' exclaimed the owner. 'Only this morning I had another monster in here asking for a mouth organ. In all my years in this shop I've never had even *one* monster buy a mouth organ and now there have been two of you in a single day. It's incredible.'
   'Yes,' smiled the monster. 'The other one must have been Armonica.'

YES – IT'S ME FOLKS

SMART ALEXANDER

What did Dr Frankenstein get when he crossed a monster with a mouse?
  Huge holes in the skirting board.

How do ghosts keep fit?
  By regular exorcise.

Why are werewolves like playing cards?
  Because they come in packs.

What did the monster say when he found he had only thistles to eat?
  Thistle have to do.

What do witches yell when they're riding in the sky?
  'Broom-Broom'.

A human being once walked into the Monster Café by mistake, bought a cup of tea and sat down. Halfway through his cuppa he noticed a werewolf watching him from a nearby table. The werewolf began to growl.

'Is he safe?' asked the man nervously.

'Well,' said the waiter, 'he's a lot safer than you are.'

How many monsters can you cram into an empty coffin?

Only one – after that it isn't empty any more.

Three very old and rather deaf monsters met in the park. 'It's windy today, isn't it?' said one.

'No, it's Thursday,' said the other.

'So am I,' said the third. 'Let's all go and have a cup of tea.'

What delivers monsters' babies?

A Frankenstork.

And what gift did the monsters give to baby Jesus?

Franken.cense.

1st Witch: Shall I buy red or black candles? Which burn longer?
2nd Witch: They both burn shorter.

How do monsters dress on a cold day?
   Quickly.

1st Cannibal: Does your wife cook best by gas or electricity?
2nd Cannibal: I don't know, I've never tried cooking her.

Why won't Count Dracula eat in restaurants?
   He's worried about getting a steak through the heart.

Count Dracula went to visit a friend of his, a vampire who had just had most of his teeth removed and was now left with just one, in the middle of his gums. 'Tell me,' asked Dracula, 'how do you cope with only one tooth?'
   'I just grin and bare it,' said the vampire.

Frankenstein's Monster: I've changed my mind.
Dr Frankenstein: Let's hope this new one works better than the old one did.

Epilaugh:
  Here lie the bones of Richard Lawton,
Whose death, alas! was strangely brought on.
Trying one day his corns to mow off,
The razor slipped and cut his toe off.
His toe, or rather, what it grew to,
An inflammation quickly flew to,
Which took, alas, to mortifying.
And that was the cause of Richard's dying.

Spook: I went to the graveyard today.
Phantom: Someone dead?
Spook: Yes, all of them.

Why did the mummy never catch cold?
  She was always well wrapped up.

Mary had a bionic cow,
It lived on safety pins.
And every time she milked that cow
The milk came out in tins.

Why do monsters eat raw meat?
  No one taught them how to cook.

Did you hear about a competition to find the laziest spook in the world? All the competitors were lined up on stage. 'I've got a really nice, easy job for the laziest person here,' said the organizer. 'Will the laziest spook raise his hand?'
  All the spooks put their hands up – except one. 'Why didn't you raise your arm?' asked the presenter.
  'Too much bother,' yawned the spook.

How do witches like to drink their tea?
  From a cup and sorceror.

Would you say that Dracula movies are fangtastic?

Two monsters were working on a building site. When lunchtime came one of them took out a box of sandwiches. 'Rat paste and tomato,' he moaned as he bit into the first. 'More rat paste and tomato,' he muttered as he ate the second.

'Rat paste and tomato?' asked his friend as he picked up the third sandwich.

'Yes,' sighed the monster. 'I hate rat paste and tomato.'

'Why don't you ask your wife to make you something different?'

The monster looked at him strangely. 'I don't have a wife – I make my sandwiches myself.'

Mummy, mummy, who don't we buy a dustbin for our rubbish?
Shut up and keep eating.

Why did the monster take a dead man for a drive in his car?
Because he was a car-case.

THERE'S THAT STUPID SOCK!

A little boy had been to play with one of his friends for the evening and stayed rather late. 'Why not stay here for the night?' suggested the friend's mother. 'We have a spare room. Come up and see.' The boy followed her up the stairs and into a gloomy-looking bedroom. In the middle of one wall was a door.

'Where does that go?' he asked.

'That goes no-where,' said his friend's mother. 'You must promise me that, whatever happens, you'll never try to open that door. Do you understand? You must never, ever open than door.'

Naturally the boy agreed, but he couldn't seem to take his eyes off the door as he got undressed and climbed into bed. Finally, forgetting what had been said, he crept out of bed and slowly pulled open the door. With a creak it opened, and the boy peered into the dark, musty-smelling room beyond. A few feet away something seemed to be moving – something shiny and slithery, which made a tapping noise as it crossed the floor in his direction. . . . Something cold and creepy, with two horrible green eyes that were watching *him*! With a cry of horror the boy raced out of the bedroom and onto the landing – and with a horrible, slithering sound, the *thing* followed.

Terrified, the boy ran downstairs and threw open the front door, then raced into the night, and all the time that horrible, slimy, rasping, nightmarish *thing* came after him. At the end of the garden was a river with a boat, and he jumped into it and began to row across, hoping, praying, that the *thing* wouldn't be able to follow him. And it didn't, because when he looked back across the river he couldn't see it anywhere. With relief he pulled the boat in to the opposite bank and sat there on the grass panting and getting his breath back. And as he sat there a horrible slimy tentacle crept out of the water, followed by the dripping *thing*, which stared at him with its hideous green eyes. 'Got you,' it hissed wickedly, and its tentacle tapped him clammily on the knee. 'Now *you're* it!'

What does Dracula say to his victims?
　It's been nice gnawing you.

What should you do if a zombie borrows your comic?
　Wait for him to give it back.

A ghost stood on the bridge one night,
Its lips were all a-quiver.
It gave a cough,
Its head fell off,
And floated down the river.

What should you call a nervous witch?
   A twitch.

Did you hear about the skeleton which was
attacked by a dog?
It ran off with some bones and left him
without a leg to stand on.

Knock, knock.
Who's there?
Dismay.
Dismay who?
*Dismay come as a surprise – I've come to eat
you!*

Did you hear about the Irish monster who
wore all his clothes to paint his house because
the label on the tin said, 'Put on three coats'?

Why did the monster take his nose apart?
   To see what made it run.

Frankenstein's Monster: They can't do my transplant this week, Dr Frankenstein doesn't have a bed free.
Igor: You'll just have to keep talking about your old operation then, won't you?

Where do ghouls go for holidays?
  Wails.

What happened after the monster ate Les Dawson?
  He felt funny.

Baby Ghost: Mummy, mummy, am I a real ghost?
Mummy Ghost: Of course you are.
Baby Ghost: Are you absolutely sure?
Mummy Ghost: Of course I am. Why?
Baby Ghost: Because I hate the dark!

Why do demons get on so well with ghouls?
  Because demons are a ghoul's best friend.

1st Ghost: I'm finding it a real bore haunting this dungeon these days.
2nd Ghost: Me too – I just can't put any life into it.

What did the undertaker say to his girlfriend?
   'Em-balmy about you.'

Did you hear about the spook who went to have a haircut? 'I'm busy,' said the barber. 'You'll have to wait.'
   'That's okay,' said the ghost. 'I'll leave me head here and call back for it later.'

A monster decided to become a TV star, so he went to see an agent. 'What do you do? asked the agent.
   'Bird impressions,' said the monster.
   'What kind of bird impressions?'
   'I eat worms.'

Spooky happenings at the supermarket! A customer was just leaning over the freezer looking for some frozen chips when ten fish fingers crept up and pulled him in . . .

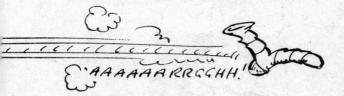

'AAAAAARRGGHH!'

It was Hallowe'en and the phantom police were on the lookout for any witches riding on their broomsticks without proper care and attention. As they watched the sky they were horrified to see a witch whiz past knitting. 'Pull over!' they called as they overtook her.

'No,' she replied, 'a pair of socks.'

Igor: Only this morning Dr Frankenstein completed another amazing operation.
He crossed an ostrich with a centipede.
Dracula: And what did he get?
Igor: We don't know – we haven't managed to catch it yet.

Why do monsters carry umbrellas?
Because umbrellas can't walk.

After years of travelling around the world in his search, the wicked Abanazar finally discovered the enchanted cave in which he believed lay the magic lamp which would make him millions. He stood before the boulders which sealed the cave and uttered the magic words, 'Open Sesame!' There was silence, and then a ghostly voice from within moaned, 'Open says-a who?'

Why is a stupid monster like the Amazon jungle?
Because they're both dense.

1st Monster: I went for a swim in the sea last summer and a shark bit off my leg.
2nd Monster: Which one?
1st Monster: No idea, they all look the same to me.

Two burglars broke into a witch's house, hoping to steal some of her magic potions. However, they'd just crept into the hallway when they heard the witch's voice saying, 'First I'm going to nibble your arms. Then I'm going to bite off your feet. Next I'm going to eat your head . . .'
With a scream of terror the two burglars fled. 'What was that?' said the witch, putting down her bag of jelly babies . . .

Did you hear the joke about the monster who climbed Nelson's Column?
Funny, neither did I . . .

Who haunted the graveyard when the spooks went on strike?
  The skeleton staff.

What should you call an admiral's ghost?
  A seal ghoul.

Why are storytellers like monsters?
  Because their tales come out of their heads.

Why do monsters have fur coats?
  They'd look silly in plastic macs, wouldn't they?

Did you hear about Smart Alec's grandfather?
It wasn't his cough that carried him off, it was the coffin they carried him off in.

Smart Alec: There's 2 monsters who serves at our local greengrocer's shop.
  He's 8 feet tall and 60 inches wide. Can you guess what he weighs?
Silly Billy: No.
Smart Alec: Vegetables.

Two monsters were out for some fresh air when one of them was run over by a lorry. 'Don't just stand there, call me an ambulance!' he cried as he lay on the ground with all five feet waving in the air.
  'All right,' said his friend. 'If it makes you feel any better, you're an ambulance!'

Did you hear about the giant monster who went shoplifting?
He got squashed under Sainsburys.

Dracula and Frankenstein's monster were stranded out in the countryside after Dracula's hearse broke down. They were ambling along a lane, picking wild flowers and wondering how many miles they were going to have to walk when a motorist in a Mini passed them and stopped. 'I can give you a lift if you like,' he told Dracula, 'but I don't have room for your big friend.'

'That's all right,' said Dracula, climbing in. 'He'll follow us.' Off went the Mini, with the driver purposely keeping the speed down to give the monster a chance to keep up. Frankenstein trotted behind without any trouble, so the car speeded up to forty and then fifty miles an hour. Still the monster ran behind without any trouble. The driver was amazed, and then he became alarmed as he noticed that Frankenstein's monster was poking his tongue out of the right side of his mouth.

'Perhaps I'd better stop,' he suggested. 'Your friend's tongue is poking out.'

'Don't worry,' said Dracula. 'It means he's going to overtake.'

Why did the little monster get into trouble for feeding the monkeys at the zoo?
   He fed them to the lions.

1st Witch: How old are you?
2nd Witch: One hundred and nine – but I don't look it, do I?
1st Witch: No, but you used to.

What do you get if you cross an Abominable Snowman with a footballer?
   I don't know, but when it tries to score a goal no one stops it.

1st Ghoul: That girl over there looks like Helen Green.
2nd Ghoul: She looks even worse in blue.

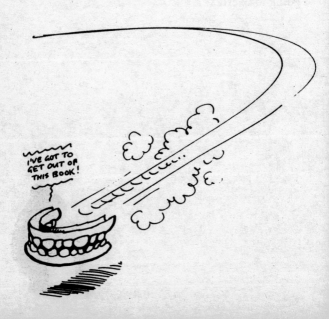

Two monsters were watching TV when Madonna appeared wearing nothing but a sexy black swimsuit. 'Hmm,' said one monster turning to the other, 'if I ever give up hating human beings I think she's the one I'd stop hating first.'

1st Monster: Why have you tied a knot in your neck?
2nd Monster: I didn't want my cold to go to my chest.

'Who's been eating my worms in slime?' asked father monster.
　'Who's been eating my minced cockroaches in diesel oil?' asked baby monster.
　'Stop complaining both of you,' yelled mother monster. 'I haven't made breakfast yet.'

A monster went shopping with sponge-fingers in one ear and jelly and custard in the other.

'Why have you got jelly and custard and sponge in your ears?' asked the shop assistant.

'You'll have to speak up,' said the monster. 'I'm a trifle deaf.'

What did the wizard say on the last day of the world?
  'Armageddon out of here.'

Did you hear about the utterly brainless monster who sat on the floor?
He fell off.

Teacher: Boris, where are the pyramids?
Boris: I don't know.
Teacher: Well where did you put them?

What happened when the Ice Monster ate a curry?
  He blew his cool.

What do you call a sorceress who stops cars with her thumb?
    A witch hiker.

1st Ghost: I'm going to France tomorrow.
2nd Ghost: By ferry?
1st Ghost: No – by hovercraft, of course!

Once upon a time there was a very ugly monster who lived a lonely, unhappy life. He longed for company, so one day he got up the courage to put an advert in the newspaper for a girlfriend. A lady did reply, and they wrote to each other several times before they decided that it was time to meet.

'I must warn you that I'm not very good-looking,' wrote the monster nervously. 'In fact I have four heads, I'm covered in nasty yellow scabs, and I've got clumps of green hair growing all over me. I also have two wooden legs and one of my arms trails along the ground when I walk. If, having heard this, you still want to meet me, I suggest we meet under the clock at King's Cross on Saturday at three.'

A couple of days later a letter came from the lady. The monster opened it with trembling fingers, terrified that his description would have put her off. 'I think personality is more important than looks,' he read, 'so I look forward to meeting you on Saturday. Would you wear a pink carnation so that I can recognize you?'

Doctor, doctor, I keep thinking I'm a ghost!
I expect that's why you just walked through that wall.

Why did the ghost's trousers fall down?
Because he had no visible means of support.

What do ghosts call the spooky navy?
The Ghost Guard.

What's the difference between a vampire and a matterbaby?
What's a matterbaby?
Nothing – what's wrong with you?

Two people went into a very dark, spooky cave. 'I can't see a thing,' said one.
'Hold my hand,' said the other.
'All right.' The first man reached out. 'Take off that horrible bristly glove first, though.'
'But I'm not wearing a glove . . .'

Igor: Is there any difference between lightning and electricity?
Dr Frankenstein: Have you ever seen a lightning bill?

What steps should you take if you're out late at night and you're followed by a thirsty vampire?
    Very big ones.

Why did the monster jump up and down?
    Because he'd just taken his medicine and he'd forgotten to shake the bottle.

'You're so ugly,' said Dracula to the witch when they were in the pub one night.
    'And you're drunk,' replied the witch.
    'Yes,' said Dracula. 'But in the morning I'll be sober.'

Did you hear about the ghost who lives in Westminster?
He's just been made spooker of the House of Lords.

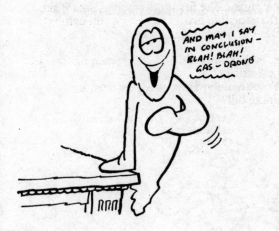

Epitaph on a gravestone:
My husband's dead and here he lies.
Nobody laughs and nobody cries.
Where he's gone or how he fares,
Nobody knows and nobody cares.

Why did the ghost leave his grave after 500 years?
   He felt he was old enough to leave home.

What happens to witches when it rains?
   They get wet.

Which murderous Victorian monster lives at the bottom of the sea?
   Jack the Kipper.

1st Vampire: Will you join me in a glass of tomato juice?
2nd Vampire: I don't think there's room for two in there.

LET ME OUT OF THIS BOOK!

Little Cannibal: I've been out hunting with my dad.
Ghoul: Catch anything?
Little Cannibal: Yes, two tourists, a missionary and a potfer.
Ghoul: What's a potfer?
Little Cannibal: To cook them in, of course.

A ghoul walked into the Monster Café and ordered a knickerbocker glory in a tall glass. When the waitress brought it to him he spooned the ice-cream out onto the floor and began to tuck into the glass. 'Yum, yum,' he said, licking his lips and putting the knobbly glass stem on the side of his plate.

A ghost who had been watching all this came over. 'What do you think you're doing?' he asked in annoyance.

'I don't like ice cream,' explained the ghoul, 'but I love glass.'

'I understand that,' said the ghost, picking up the glass stem from the plate, 'But why are you leaving the best bit?'

Igor: There's a question I'd like to ask you, Count Dracula.
Dracula: Go ahead.
Igor: Why do you always chew mints?
Dracula: Strictly between you and me, Igor, I suffer from bat breath.

Monster: I'm going to have to stop going out with that dragon.

Ghost: Why? He's hot stuff.

Monster: I know, but every time we kiss he steams my glasses up.

Two old ladies were looking at a mummy on display in the British Museum. '1000 BC,' read one of them aloud, looking at the sign on the case. 'What does that mean?'

'I expect it's the number of the car that ran him over,' said the other.

Dr Frankenstein: How did you get that splinter in your finger?

Monster: I scratched my head.

Which spook pulls horrid faces at Han Solo and Luke Skywalker?
   Princess Leer.

Two villains heard that an old lady had just died and been buried in the churchyard, and that a very valuable diamond ring had been buried with her on her finger. They decided to open the grave and dig it up, and this gruesome task they completed. But try as they might they couldn't remove the beautiful ring from her finger. 'I'll have to chop her finger off,' said one of the robbers, and he did.

When they'd finished their horrible task they looked around for somewhere to spend the night before they made their escape. The only place seemed to be a very big, eerie old house with a sign up offering Bed and Breakfast. They went up the front steps and knocked, and a hideous old lady opened the door and let them in. 'Would you like a hot drink before you go to bed?' she asked them.

'Oh yes,' they said, and followed her into a dusty old kitchen. As she poured them a cup of tea they noticed that she had one finger missing. 'How did you lose your finger?' one of the villains asked curiously.

The old lady seemed to flicker before their eyes, and she turned a terrible red-eyed gaze on them. 'It was cut off,' she moaned, 'and you've got it in your pocket . . .'

How do monsters dress on a cold day?
  Quickly.

Monster: You've got a simple choice. Give me your money or I'll eat you up.
Smart Alec: You'd better eat me – I'm saving my money for my old age.

What do you call an Irishman who is dug up after 100 years?
  Pete.

Where do you find monster snails?
  At the end of monster's fingers.

What's huge and hairy and red and hides in corners?
  An embarrassed monster.

Why do sorcerors drink lots of tea?
  Because sorcerors need cuppas.

*What do green, hairy-bottomed monsters have
that no one else has?*
  Baby green, hairy-bottomed monsters.

1st Cannibal: My husband's always moaning.
2nd Cannibal: So is mine. To hear him go on
you'd think he already had one foot in the
gravy.

Knock, knock.
  Who's there?
Ammonia.
  Ammonia who?
*Ammonia little vampire and I can't reach the
bell.*

Why are ghouls always poor?
  Because a ghoul and his money are soon
parted.

What kind of mistakes do spooks make?
  Boo-boos.

Smart Alec: What's green and shiny, has yellow fangs, little red eyes and twenty purple hairy legs?
Silly Billy: I don't know. What is it?
Smart Alec: I don't know either, but there's one crawling up your leg.

Why couldn't Dracula's wife get to sleep?
  Because of his coffin.

A sea monster who saw an oil tanker,
Munched a hole in the side and then sank her.
It swallowed the crew
In a minute or two,
And then picked its teeth with the anchor.

What is the monsters' favourite ballet?
  Swamp Lake.

Who appears on the front of ghostly magazines?
  The cover ghoul.

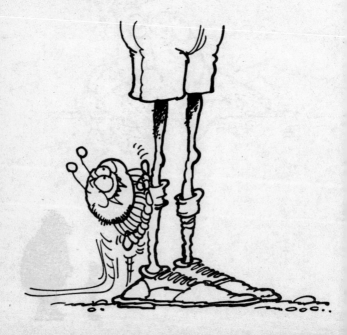

Why do mummies make excellent spies?
    They're good at keeping things under
wraps.

A young man of chill Aberdeen,
Once grew so remarkably lean,
So flat and compressed,
That his back touched his chest,
And sideways he couldn't be seen.

Ghoul Nurse: How many patients has Dr
Frankenstein seen this afternoon?
    Two?
Ghost Nurse: No, three. I've taken them all to
the morgue.

*Why did the skeleton refuse to go to the
cinema?*
    Because his heart wasn't in it.

The undertaker and his assistants were trying to load a coffin containing a dead monster into the hearse. As the monster was 3 metres long it was very difficult. They staggered down the steps, got one end into the car, but just as they'd wedged the coffin almost in place one of the assistants let go and it fell to the floor. 'This is no good,' said the undertaker. 'We'll have to re-hearse it now!'

1st Witch: A werewolf bit me on the leg last night.
2nd Witch: Did you put anything on it?
1st Witch: No, it must have tasted okay as it was.

What did the monster do when his wife turned into a pillar of salt?
    He put her in the cellar.

What is black and has eight wheels?
    A witch on roller skates.

What soup do Irish cannibals like best?
  The broth of a boy.

Monster: Do you have many church bells in Paris?
Hunchback of Notre Dame: About two hundred, all tolled.

What's 30 metres tall and goes 'eef, if, of, muf?'
  A backward giant.

Why did the huge horrible monster go to see the psychiatrist?
  Because he was worried that people liked him.

1st Witch: I'm terribly sorry. I just cast the wrong spell and I turned your black cat into an elephant. Can I replace him?
2nd Witch: Are you any good at catching mice?

How do monsters pass through locked doors?
   They use skeleton keys.

What shows do ghosts go to at Christmas?
   Phantomimes.

Smart Alec: I just bought a haunted bicycle.
Silly Billy: How do you know it's haunted?
Smart Alec: It's got lots of spooks in its wheels.

LET ME OUT OF THIS BOOK!

Mummy Monster: Just run into the house dear and collect the knives and forks, the salt and pepper, and the tomato sauce.
Little Monster: Why, mummy?
Mummy Monster: Your little brother's just fallen on the barbecue.

Why do witches ride broomsticks around central London?
 Have you ever seen a broomstick with a wheel clamp?

What did the witch and the wizard eat for lunch?
 Toads in the hole.

1st Monster: I wish I had a penny for every man who's asked me to marry him.
2nd Monster: Yes, you could buy a packet of mints then, couldn't you?

Did you hear about the monster who was put together upside down?
 His nose runs and his feet smell.

Which is a ghost's favourite lake?
 Lake Eerie.

*How should you address the Lord High
Ghost?*
Your Ghostliness.
*And how should you address the Lord High
Monster?*
Your Ghastliness.

A rabbit hopped into a country pub and
jumped up onto the counter. 'Have you got
anything to eat?' he asked the surprised
landlord.

'Well, yes,' said the landlord. 'Actually we
have a very special line in new Toasties – but
we don't normally serve rabbits.'

'Oh, please,' begged the rabbit. 'I'm
starving.' The landlord agreed, and the rabbit
ordered half a pint of shandy and a toastie.

'What sort of toastie would you like? We've
got cheese toasties, mushroom toasties, ham
toasties, tomato toasties, salmon toasties,
baked bean toasties and chicken toasties.'

The rabbit ordered a tomato toastie and
when it came he ate it up, then hopped up to
the bar and ordered a cheese toastie and a
ham toastie. He ate these up too, and ordered
a chicken toastie and a salmon one. 'You'll
burst,' joked the landlord, but the rabbit ate
them all, paid his bill and hopped off.

Later that day the landlord opened for
business again – and into his bar hopped the
ghost of the rabbit. It jumped up onto the
counter and looked at him soulfully with its
little red eyes. 'Aaah!' cried the landlord.
'What happened? Where you run over by a
car? Did a fox get you?'

'No,' whispered the rabbit ghost, 'I died of
mixin' ma toasties.'

What kind of beans do cannibals like best?
   Human beans.

1st Ghoul: My son's very keen on long walks
in the country.
2nd Ghoul: He's a fresh air fiend, is he?

*What did the monster say when he saw Father
Christmas?*
   'Yum, yum!'

*Mummy, mummy, teacher keeps saying I look
like a werewolf.*
   Be quiet dear and go and comb your face.

What's the difference between a vampire and a biscuit?
  You can't dip a vampire in your tea.

'I'm going to eat you up,' said the werewolf to the vicar who had been silly enough to take a short cut through the haunted wood.
  'Help me, Lord!' cried the vicar.
  The werewolf fell to its knees and began to pray fervently. 'It's a miracle!' declared the vicar.
  'No, it's not,' replied the werewolf. 'I'm just saying grace.'

Why did the lady monster wear a bikini to the office?
  Because she was in the typing pool.

Is Dracula good at cricket?
  He's not a brilliant fielder, but he's a great bats-man.

*Did you hear about the monster who was
known as Captain Kirk?*
   He had a left ear, a right ear and a final
   front ear.

1st Ghost: You can tell that spook over there
was a good driver when he was alive.
2nd Ghost: How do you know that?
1st Ghost: He's asked to be fitted with wing
mirrors.

*What did one of Frankenstein's ears say to the
other ear?*
   I didn't know we were living on the same
   block!

Did you hear about the lady monster who was
so determined to be beautiful that she put on
vanishing cream, anti-wrinkle cream,
moisturising lotion and vitamin E cream? It
didn't work, though. In fact it turned her
black and blue, because every night she kept
sliding out of bed.

1

1st Monster: I used to work with hundreds of people under me.
2nd Monster: You? Never!
1st Monster: I did – I was a gardener in a cemetery.

Why was the ghost arrested?
  He didn't have a haunting licence.

How do you get ten huge hairy monsters in a matchbox?
  First take out all the matches.

Mrs Monster: I don't know what to buy my husband for Christmas.
Mrs Spook: How about some nice Brute aftershave?

COR – AFTER SHAVE!

Monster Dad: I've just become a father and the baby looks just like me!
Ghost: Oh well, as long as it's healthy . . .

A monster walked into a pub and asked the landlord, 'Do you serve Germans?'

'Of course,' said the landlord. 'I'm not prejudiced.'

'I'll have a glass of lemonade and two Germans in that case,' said the monster.

Did you hear about the monster burglar who fell in the cement mixer?

Now he's a hardened criminal.

What did the cannibal say when he met the famous explorer?

Dr Livingstone, I consume?

1st Monster: We had burglars last night.
2nd Monster: Nice?
1st Monster: Yes, but not as nice as the shepherds pie the night before.

When does a ghost become two ghosts?
  When he's beside himself.

What goes, 'Grrr! Grrr! Bang!'
  A monster in a minefield.

Ghost: Did you hear the new deodorant called Vanish?
Spook: Does it work?
Ghost: It's brilliant. You spray it on and disappear – then no one knows where the smell is coming from.

What did the ghoul say to the zombie?
   'Hello, Zombie . . .'

A hairy monster walked into the chemist's
shop. 'Don't your toes go blue, walking about
with nothing on your feet?' asked the girl
behind the counter.
   'Oh,' said the monster looking down at his
feet. 'I thought I was in Boots.'

*Why isn't it a good idea to play jokes on the
snake monster?*
   Because you can never pull its legs.

*Why did the monster cowboy take a sledge-
hammer to bed?*
   He wanted to hit the hay.

What is always higher than a giant?
   His hat.

How did the monster pirate show affection?
   He hugged the shore.

Two monsters from outer space landed their
spacecraft in the countryside very late one
night, and the first thing they saw was a
telephone box.
   'Take me to your leader,' said the first
monster.
   'Don't be silly,' said the other, 'can't you
see he's only a baby?'

Werewolf: I just swallowed a bus!
Monster: Are you choking?
Werewolf: No, I really did!

*Why was the ghost policeman surprised when
his girlfriend was arrested for burglary?*
   He didn't suspectre.

ARREST
THAT
JOKE!

GRAVE
VOICE!

1st Ghostbuster: There's a strange knocking noise – it must be a ghost!
2nd Ghostbuster: No, it's my knees.

Three young men who all wanted to get on in the world visited their local witch to see if she could help them. 'We'd all like to have good careers and make a lot of money,' they explained.

'That's easy,' said the witch. 'All you have to do is spend an hour in my dismal dungeon and you will be granted one wish. The first thing you say will come true, so be very careful.'

The first young man entered the dismal dungeon and as he opened the door he was greeted by the most terrible smell in the world – a smell of dead cats, rotting cabbage, blocked-up drains, and heaps of manure. It was horrible! 'I wish to be a solicitor', he choked. And when he staggered out an hour later he was dressed in a smart pin-striped suit and carrying a briefcase which contained his legal qualifications.

The second man ventured in holding his nose. 'I wish to be a champion athlete,' he gasped. And when he emerged after an hour he was wearing shorts and t-shirt and looked every inch an athlete.

The third man opened the dungeon door and stepped in bravely. 'I want . . . Pooh!' he cried as the smell hit him. And straightaway he was turned into a bear . . .

Spook Teacher: What do you want to be when you grow up?
Little Spook: An air ghostess.

Where do ghosts go for their holidays?
  The East Ghost.

A disgusting old monster from Twickenham
Had boots too tight to walk quickenham.
He walked for a mile,
And stopped with a smile,
Then pulled off his boots and was sickenham.

Igor: What would you get if you crossed a monster with a carnation?
Dr Frankenstein: I don't know, but I wouldn't try smelling it.

1st Monster: I weighed myself this morning.
2nd Monster: And how much do you weigh?
1st Monster: Two stone.
2nd Monster: But you're eight feet tall and very fat.
1st Monster: All right – I'll admit the needle went round three times . . .

Five huge hairy monsters all stood under one teensy-weensy umbrella and none of them got wet. Why?
   It wasn't raining.

Smart Alec: I've just met a monster with no nose.
Silly Billy: Really? How did he smell?
Smart Alec: Awful.

Why won't the skeleton have a bath?
   He's scared of slipping down the plughole.

Girl Monster: Do you love me?
Boy Monster: Yes, I'd die for you.
Girl Monster: You keep promising that but you never do.

Which ghost wears thermal and lurex underwear?
   The ghost of Long John Silver.

What did the ghost give his wife for Christmas?
    A corset, so that she could retain her
    ghoulish figure.

What did the six-footed monster use for his flat feet?
    A foot pump.

1st Monster: My grandfather had three
wooden legs.
2nd Monster: Well, my grandfather had two
oak chests.

What did the cannibal say after he'd spent the day fishing?
    I haven't had a bite all day.

A big-mouthed little red monster went up to Dracula. 'What do you like to eat, Count Dracula?' he asked.

'Human blood,' said the Count.

'And what do you like to eat, Mrs Witch?' asked the big-mouthed little red monster.

'Frogs and snails,' said the witch.

The little red big-mouthed monster went up to the big blue monster. 'What do you like to eat, Mr Blue Monster?'

'Big-mouthed little red monsters,' replied the big blue monster.

'Oh,' said the big-mouthed little red monster. (Keep your mouth shut and speak quietly when you say this) 'You don't see many of those around here.'

Sign seen at school:
These are the graves of three poor sinners,
Who died after eating our school dinners.

Did you hear about the time the Irish monster was hitch-hiking to the south of France? A motorist stopped for him and asked if he wanted a lift.

'Oui, oui,' said the monster in his best French.

'Not in the back of my car you don't,' said the motorist, driving off.

1st Witch: I'm suffering from terrible hypnotism.
2nd Witch: You can't suffer from hypnotism.
1st Witch: Yes you can – rheumatism of the hip.

Did you hear about the witch who fed her pet vulture on sawdust? The vulture laid ten eggs and when they hatched, nine chicks had wooden legs and the tenth was a woodpecker.

Did you hear about the monster who ate nothing but plastic foam?
He went soft in the head.

How many letters are there in the alphabet?
   Only twenty-four – E.T. went home.

Who is the only driver who doesn't suffer from backseat drivers?
   An undertaker driving a hearse.

Monster: I'm so ugly.
Ghost: It's not that bad!
Monster: It is! When my grandfather was born they passed out cigars. When my father was born they just passed out cigarettes. When I was born they simply passed out.

What did the man-eating monster call his new baby?
   Norah.

What kind of monster is it safe to put in the washing-machine?
   A wash-and-wear-wolf.

The ghost teacher was giving her pupils instructions on how to haunt a house properly. 'Has everyone got the hang of walking through walls?' she asked. One little ghoul at the front of the class looked uncertain.
   'Just watch the blackboard everyone,' instructed the teacher, 'and I'll go through it once more.'

Why are undertakers happy when people die?
   Because every shroud has a silver lining.

THERE'S A GHOST IN THIS BOOK!

Why did the cannibal buy a hammer?
  To knock the tops off his boiled heads.

Dracula: Don't be frightened, I don't have an enemy in the world.
Victim: No, they're all in the next!

Why was the sword-swallowing monster put in prison?
  He coughed and killed two people.

Frankenstein's Monster: My wife's just joined the Women's Movement. Life's not worth living.
Dracula: Why not?
Frankenstein's Monster: She's so independent. Its Lib this and Lib that. She even drinks Libber-tea.

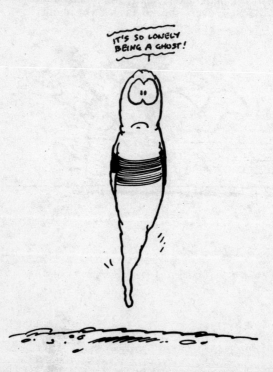

When is it bad luck to have a black cat follow you?
    When you're a mouse.

Witch: Will you still love me when I'm old and ugly?
Wizard: But I already do!

A mother monster marched her naughty little monster into the doctor's surgery. 'Is it possible that he could have taken his own tonsils out?' she asked.
    'No,' said the doctor.
    'I told you so,' said the mother monster. 'Now put them back this minute.'

Why did the cyclops apply·for half a television licence?
    Because he only had one eye.

1st Witch: I'm so unlucky.
2nd Witch: Why, what's happened?
1st Witch: I met a handsome prince at a New Year's Eve party, but when I kissed him he turned into a frog.

Witch: How much are your black candles?
Shopkeeper: A pound each.
Witch: That's candleous!

Igor: Why are you lying down flat?
Dr Frankenstein: Yesterday I crossed a dive and a handstand.
Igor: And what did you get?
Dr Frankenstein: A broken back.

1st Witch: There's a small slug in my salad!
2nd Witch: I'm so sorry – I'll take it away and get you a larger one.

What's the first thing ghosts do when they get into a car?
They boo-kle their seatbelts.

Boy Monster: I think you wear too much make-up.
Girl Monster: But I have to make myself look more beautiful.
Boy Monster: It's so thick that your face is still smiling ten minutes after you've stopped laughing.

Smart Alec: Last summer I went ghost-hunting in the Arctic. I caught fifty.
Silly Billy: But there aren't any ghosts in the Arctic!
Smart Alec: Of course not. I caught them all.

Igor: Dr Frankenstein, I'm worried about my brother. He thinks he's a lift.
Dr Frankenstein: Send him up and I'll have a word with him.
Igor: I can't, he doesn't stop at this floor.

1st Witch: My dustbin must be full of toadstools.
2nd Witch: Why's that?
1st Witch: There's not mushroom inside.

The monster from outer space decided to go on a trip around the universe, so he went to the rocket office to book a ticket to the moon. 'Sorry, sir,' said the attendant, 'the moon is full at the moment.'

What did the werewolf write at the bottom of his letter?
    Best vicious . . .

Did you hear about the lady ghoul who went to buy a dress in the Phantom Fashion boutique?
    'I'd like to try on that shroud in the window,' she told the ghoul in charge.
    'Yes, madam,' said the ghoul, 'but wouldn't you prefer to use the changing-room instead?'

Smart Alec: Would you say that someone with four hands was a monster?
Silly Billy: Yes, I would.
Smart Alec: You're a monster then.
Silly Billy: But I don't have four hands!
Smart Alec: When you double your fists you do.

Why was the cannibal expelled from school?
  Because he kept buttering up the teacher.

What's green, has six legs and kills people by jumping on them from trees?
  The phantom snooker table.

What happened when Dr Frankenstein swallowed some uranium?
  He got atomic ache.

A monster went to see the doctor because he kept bumping into things. 'You need glasses,' said the doctor.

'Will I be able to read with them?' asked the monster.

'Yes.'

'That's brilliant,' said the monster. 'I didn't know how to before!'

What's a ghoul's favourite dish?
  Ghoulash.

Superman climbed to the top of a high mountain in the middle of the African jungle. As he reached the summit he found himself suddenly surrounded by dozens of vicious vampires and ghosts and monsters and goblins. What did he say?
  'Boy, am I in the wrong joke!'

Smart Alec: Why do you call your husband laryngitis?
Countess Dracula: Because he's a pain in the neck.

Did you hear about the stupid monster who hurt himself while he was out raking up leaves?
He fell out of a tree.

1st Monster: Do you like Kipling?
2nd Monster: I don't know, I've never kippled.

How do witches tell the time?
  By their witch watches.

How do worried ghosts look?
  Grave.

A monster and a zombie went into the undertaker's. 'I'd like to order a coffin for a friend of mine who has just died,' said the monster.
  'Certainly, sir,' said the undertaker, 'but there was really no need to bring him here with you.'

1st Werewolf: Nerg.
2nd Werewolf: Nerg, nerg, yug.
1st Werewolf: Don't start changing the subject.

Did you hear the story about the Irish vampire? He went out for a bite late one night and was walking home when he stumbled over an old kettle lying on the ground. And when he kicked it into the gutter there was a sudden blinding flash of light and a green genie appeared.

'Greetings,' said the genie. 'I am the green genie and I will grant you three wishes.'

The vampire thought for a few seconds. 'What I'd really like,' he said, 'is a big bottle of blood that never empties, no matter how much I drink from it.'

'Alla kazaaam!' zapped the genie. There was another flash of light and, sure enough, a bottle of blood appeared. The vampire took a long drink. 'Yum, yum,' he said. 'And look, the bottle's still full to the brim! This is marvellous!'

'I can't hang around all night,' complained the genie. 'What are your other two wishes?'

The vampire thought for a minute before saying, 'I'll have two more bottles like this.'

1st Ghost: How did you get that terrible bump on your head?
2nd Ghost: I was floating through a keyhole when some idiot put the key in the lock.

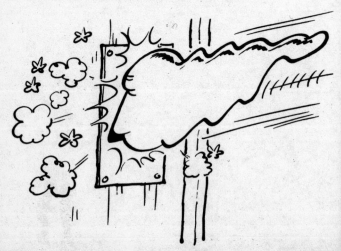

Two monsters came to lay a carpet in a witch's house. 'I'm off for a spell,' she told them. 'Be back soon.'

When the monsters had finished they noticed a small bump in the middle of the carpet. 'Must be my cigarettes,' said one monster. And rather than taking up the whole carpet and starting all over again, he took a huge mallet and squashed the lump flat.

Just then the witch came back. 'I found your cigarettes lying on the path outside,' she said, handing the packet to the monster. 'By the way, I've lost my toad. You haven't seen him anywhere have you?'

Why did Frankenstein's monster stop smoking?
He had his fuse box repaired.

Frankenstein's Monster: I hate Father's Day.
Igor: Why?
Frankenstein's Monster: I have to buy 14 Father's Day cards.

Monster: I used to be a werewolf.
Smart Alec: Really?
Werewolf: Yes, but I'm all right noooo-ooo-ooo-ooow!

The stupid monster went to the mind reader's and paid £5 to have his thoughts read. After half an hour the mind reader gave him his money back.

1st Witch: My hovel's getting so bad I can hardly live in it. And yesterday the roof sprung a leak.
2nd Witch: Won't the council fix it for you?
1st Witch: Fix it? They want to charge me extra rent for the use of a shower!

Two ghouls were in the middle of an argument. 'I didn't come here to be insulted,' yelled one.
    'Really? Where do you usually go?'

What did the policeman say to the three-headed burglar?
    All, allo, allo.

Little Billie's dead
So bung him in a coffin.
We don't get the chance
Of a funeral of'en.

1st Witch: Why do you put birdseed in your shoes?
2nd Witch: I've got pigeon toes.

The ghost teacher was giving a lesson about monsters. 'And which family does the Abominable Snowman belong to?' she asked the class.
  'I don't know,' replied one pupil. 'No one in our road has got one.'

Why are Dracula's friends crazy?
  Because they're all bats.

What do you get if you cross an official on a train and a ghost?
  A ticket inspectre.

Smart Alec: What's the difference between a vampire and a letterbox?
Silly Billy: I don't know.
Smart Alec: I'm not going to send you to post a letter then!

Why doesn't it cost much to take Dracula out for dinner?

Because he eats necks to nothing.

It was a dark and stormy night when little Justin's parents went out. 'Are you sure you'll be all right, dear?' they asked.

'Of course I will,' snapped Justin. But no sooner had the front door slammed behind them than the telephone rang. 'I am the ghost of Bleeding Toe, and I'm on my way to see you,' groaned a creepy voice when Justin answered. 'I'll be there in two minutes!' Poor Justin dropped the telephone in fright. What was he going to do?

He bolted the front door, then ran upstairs to hide in his bedroom. There was a big cupboard in the corner of the room, so he climbed in there and pulled the door shut behind him. But it was too late. Already he could hear a hideous sound of heavy, dragging footsteps coming up the stairs after him. Shaking with terror he waited in the cupboard. There was a terrible crash as the thing pushed down his bedroom door and came into the room. Justin could hear it sniffing and listening for him – and then suddenly the door of the cupboard was wrenched off its hinges and he was confronted by the hideous sight of a huge, shaggy monster with staring red eyes and, most horrible of all,
a trail of blood stretching across the carpet.

'What do you want?' screamed Justin, quaking with fear.

The ghost paused, then moaned in its sepulchral voice, 'I am Bleeding Toe. Would you put a plaster on my foot, please?'

What did Queen Victoria say when she saw the ghost of Charles I?
  You must be off your head!

Which country do abominable snowmen come from?
  Chile.

Did you receive an invitation to the zombie's party? It read: Please come to my party in the graveyard at midnight, where I'm digging up some old friends . . .

Dracula: Why did you drive straight into my car?
Motorist: Well, you had a sign saying 'Give Blood' in your back window, so I thought you could have some of mine.

What's the definition of a cannibal?
   A man who goes to a restaurant and orders
   the waiter.

Cross-eyed Monster: When I grow up I want
to be a bus driver.
Witch: Well, I won't stand in your way.

What happens if you're good in this life?
   You get everlasting bliss.
And what happens if you're bad in this life?
   You get everlasting blisters.

What do ghosts do at 11 a.m.?
   They take a coffin break.

Smart Alec: I just met the demon body-snatchers.
Silly Billy: What happened?
Smart Alec: I nearly got carried away!

A ghost was out haunting one night and met a fairy fluttering through the forest. 'Hallo,' said the ghost. 'I've never met a fairy before. What's your name?'

'Nuff,' said the fairy.

'That's a very odd name,' said the ghost.

'No it's not,' said the fairy, offended. 'Haven't you heard of Fairy Nuff?'

Why are monsters huge and hairy and ugly?
   Because if they were small and round and smooth they'd be Smarties.

Boy Monster: You've got a face like a million dollars!
Girl Monster: Have I really?
Boy Monster: Yes, it's all green and wrinkly.

What happened to the man who refused to pay his exorcist's bill?
  He was repossessed.

Where do gnomes and fairies and goblins always go at the end of the day?
  Gnome, sweet gnome.

What are miniatures?
  Small vampires eating toffees.

A horrible ugly old witch surprised all her friends by announcing that she was going to get married. 'But,' said another old hag, 'you always said men were stupid. And you vowed never to marry.'
  'Yes, I know,' said the witch. 'But I finally found one who asked me.'

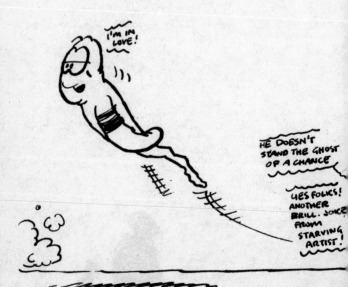

What did the mad axeman's wife say in November?
> Only thirty chopping days to Christmas, dear.

Little Monster: My dad's so huge he dug the hole for Lake Windermere all on his own.
Little Ghoul: Well my dad's so strong he killed the Dead Sea.

Did you hear about the girl monster who wasn't pretty and wasn't ugly?
> She was pretty ugly.

Frankenstein had a wristwatch;
He swallowed it one day.
So now he's taking Beecham's Pills
To pass the time away.

Mummy, mummy, I hate Daddy's guts. *
> Be quiet and eat what's on the plate.

* THIS SHOULD BE IN 'SMART ALEC'S REVOLTING JOKES FOR KIDS' BUT IT'S NOT QUITE HORRIBLE ENOUGH!

Knock knock.
  Who's there?
Ivan
  Ivan who?
Ivan to hear you scream!

What did the pub landlord say to the ghost?
  Sorry, but we don't serve spirits here.

What kind of monster has the best hearing?
  The eeriest.

How can you tell if you've had a monster in your fridge?
  It leaves footprints in the butter.

Why did the vampire jump on a tomato?
  Because he felt like playing squash.

Monster: You dance so well, my dear.
Witch: I wish I could say the same for you.
Monster: You could if you were as big a liar as
I am.

A little monster was learning to play the
violin. 'I'm good, aren't I? he asked his big
brother.
  'You should be on the radio,' said the
brother.
  'You think I'm *that* good?'
  'No, I think you're terrible, but at least if
you were on the radio I could switch you off.'

Would you say that a cannibal who ate his
mother's sister was an aunt-eater?

1st Cannibal: My dad's so tough he can kill crocodiles with his bare hands.

2nd Cannibal: *My* dad's so tough it took six hours in the microwave to cook him.

What happened when the ghostly cows got out of their field?
    There was udder chaos.

1st Cannibal: How did you know that the vicar has been eaten?

2nd Cannibal: Let's just say that I have inside information.

1st Cannibal: I think all these cannibal jokes are in poor taste!

1st Monster: That orange and red checked coat of yours is a bit loud!

2nd Monster: It's okay when I put on my muffler.

A little boy came downstairs crying late one night. 'What's wrong?' asked his mother.

'Do people really come from dust, like they said in church?' he sobbed.

'In a way they do,' said his mother.

'And when they die do they turn back into dust?'

'Yes, they do.'

The little boy began to cry again. 'Well, under my bed there's someone either coming or going!'

1st Ghost: Have you read the Bible?
2nd Ghost: No, I'm waiting for the video.

1st Monster: What's that growing out of your ears?
2nd Monster: Spinach.
1st Monster: That's terrible!
2nd Monster: I know, I planted carrots.

A monster heard her children scream
So she pushed them in the stream
Saying, as she pushed the third,
'Children should be seen, not heard.'

What kind of planes do dragons fly?
  Spitfires.

Where do monsters with terrible coughs go every evening?
  To the theatre.

What kind of coat does a six-handed monster wear?
  A coat of arms.

Did you hear about the monster who swallowed a lightbulb?
  He spat it out and now he's delighted.

Why did the lady monster dip her head in a can of paint?
    To see if blondes have more fun.

What do the Ice Monsters call their babies?
    Chill-dren.

1st Cannibal: The doctor's told me to go on a diet.
2nd Cannibal: What are you allowed to eat?
1st Cannibal: Midgets.

Hairy Monster: I've traced my family all the way back to royalty.
Witch: King Kong?

How do you make a thin monster fat?
  Throw him over a cliff and he'll come down 'plump'.

What should you expect if you call on a witch at lunchtime?
  Pot luck.

What's the best way to raise an abandoned baby monster?
  With a fork-lift truck.

1st Monster: My wife sleeps under the bed.
2nd Monster: Why does she do that?
1st Monster: I think she's a little potty.

What did the monsters give the undertaker and the snake charmer when they were married?
  'Hiss' and 'Hearse' bath towels.

Dr Frankenstein: I've just completed my latest experiment!
Igor: What did you do?
Dr Frankenstein: I crossed a duck and a whale.
Igor: And what did you get?
Dr Frankenstein: Moby Duck!

When is a vampire likely to enter the house?
  When the door is left open.

1st Witch: Your toad keeps bumping into things.
2nd Witch: Yes, he needs glasses.
1st Witch: Why not send him to the hoptician?

What's a monster's favourite pudding?
  Ice scream.

What happens if a huge, hairy monster sits in front of you at the pictures?
  You miss most of the movie.

Smart Alec: I've just tricked Dracula out of £100!
Silly Billy: How did you do that?
Smart Alec: It's easy – he's a real sucker.

Why did the ghost scratch himself?
  He was the only one who knew where it itched.

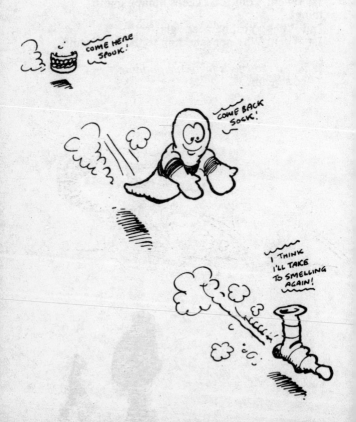

Monster: Doctor, I can't help pulling ugly
  faces.
Doctor: Don't worry, it's not serious.
Monster: But the people with the ugly faces
  don't like it when I pull them . . .

Why is Dr Frankenstein never lonely?
  He can always make friends.

There once was a young ghost from
  Gloucester,
Whose parents imagined they'd lost her.
From the fridge came a sound
And at last she was found.
But the problem was how to defrost her.

Dr Frankenstein: I fancy something tasty for
lunch. I think I'll cross a saucepan of stew
with a famous cowboy.
Igor: What will that make?
Dr Frankenstein: Hopalong Casserole.

What happened when vampires took over at the waterboard?

There were bloodbaths everywhere.

What did the baby ghost call his mum and dad?

Transparents.

Smart Alec: I just met a zombie!
Silly Billy: Did you have a nice chat?
Smart Alec: No, I can't speak dead languages.

What is the best way to speak to an abominable snowman?

From a very long distance.

What knots do undertakers use?
  Wreath knots.

*How do monster snowmen feel when they
begin to melt?*
  Abominable.

1st Witch: My boyfriend loves me so much he
calls me Wonder Woman.
2nd Witch: That's because he wonders
whether you're a woman or not.

Young Ghoul: This unemployment is terrible!
Ghost: I know – but I've got just the job for
you.
Young Ghoul: What is it?
Ghost: All you have to do is go round scaring
people out of their hiccups.

Why did the ghost go into the chemist shop?
  To collect his film transparencies.

Why is a werewolf in your house like a chauffeur?
  Both drive you away.

1st Monster: That girl over there just rolled her eyes at you.
2nd Monster: Roll them back then.

Smart Alec: Would you and the other skeletons like to run a stall at our village fête?
Skeleton: Yes, we'll do the rattle.

1st Monster: My husband's manners have really improved.
2nd Monster: Why is that?
1st Monster: He's taken a job in a refinery.
2nd Monster: My husband's very polite too.
1st Monster: Really?
2nd Monster: Yes, he always takes his shoes off before he puts his feet up on the table.

What newspapers do hangmen read?
   Noosepapers.

What did the hippie monster say to the invisible spirit?
   You're out of sight, man.

The man who makes me does not need me. The man who buys me does not use me himself. The man who needs me doesn't know he needs me and he never sees me. What am I?
   A coffin.

1st Monster: Mrs Tremble's just out of hospital.

2nd Monster: She had her ghoul stones removed, didn't she?

1st Monster: Yes, and she can't stop talking about her apparition.

Do skeletons have good boxers?
    No, they don't have the guts.

1st Monster: I can't think what to get my husband for Christmas.

2nd Monster: Do the same as me and get him three pairs of gloves for his hands.

Why does Dracula always travel with his coffin?
    Because his life is at stake.

How do you join the Dracula fan club?
  Just send your name, address and blood
  group.

*What do you get if a huge hairy monster steps
on Batman and Robin?*
  Flatman and Ribbon.

What did one dragon say to the other dragon?
  I keep trying to give up smoking but I can't.

*Which ghost sailed the seven seas looking for
rubbish and blubber?*
  The ghost of Binbag the Whaler.

Ugly Monster: Isn't it odd how many girls these days don't want to get married?
Monster: What makes you say that?
Ugly Monster: I've asked all of them and they've said the same thing . . .

What should you do if you find that your bedroom is haunted?
   Move house.

What made Joan Collins marry a ghost?
   She didn't know what possessed her.

A monster walked into a hamburger restaurant and ordered a cheese burger, fries and a chocolate milkshake. When he finished his meal he left a £10 to pay the bill. The waiter, thinking that the monster probably wasn't very good at adding up, gave him only 50p change.

   At that moment another customer came in. 'Gosh,' he said, seeing the monster. 'I've never seen a monster in here before.'

   'And you won't be seeing me again,' said the monster furiously, 'not at these prices.'

What walks through walls backwards, goes pink and says, 'Excuse me . . . er, boo!'
   A shy ghost.

Two ghostly pigeons were sitting in the belfry of the haunted church. Suddenly another phantom pigeon flew past them. 'Did you see that?' asked one pigeon, amazed.
   'See what?' asked the other.
   'That pigeon was people-toed!'

What did the bald monster say when he was given a comb?
   Thank you – I'll never part with it.

Did you hear about the stupid vampire who listened to a match?
   He burned his ear.

THAT'S THE TROUBLE WITH GHOST JOKES! NO DOGS!

Two monsters were in hospital and they were discussing their operations and ailments.
'Have you had your feet checked?' one asked the other.

'No,' came the reply. 'They've always been purple with green spots.'

What's huge and green and sits in the corner moaning all day?
The Incredible Sulk.

What do you call an 8-foot tall monster covered in green slime and with half a loaf of bread in each ear?
Anything you like, because he can't hear you.

Why did the monster at the bottom of the sea blush?
Because he saw the Queen Elizabeth's bottom.

What was the ghost's favourite TV programme?
    Horro-nation Street.

What flies around wearing a black cape and sucking people's blood?
    A mosquito in a cape.

Mrs Monster: I've stopped my son biting his nails.
Phantom: How did you do that?
Mrs Monster: I knocked his teeth out.

Smart Alec: Did you hear about the eight stupid monsters? They were called Do, Re, Fa, So, La, Ti, Do . . .
Silly Billy: What about Mi?
Smart Alec: Sorry, I forgot about you!

Did you hear about the Irish monster who went to night school to learn to read in the dark?

HOW ABOUT A VAMPIRE?

1st Toad: My witch is busy making yoghurt.
2nd Toad: How does she do it?
1st Toad: She just buys a pint of milk and stares at it.

Dr Frankenstein: I think I'll cover my latest monster creation with gold paint.
Igor: Don't do that, Doctor, you'll give him a gilt complex.

What did the camper feel when he realized that his sleeping bag was haunted?
   Intense fear.

1st Witch: My boyfriend thinks I have a complexion like peaches and cream.
2nd Witch: A rotten peach and sour cream?

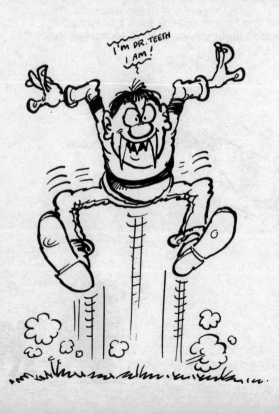

Two Irish zombies went looking for work at the Job Centre. The first one went for an interview and was told he would be given a simple intelligence test. 'What is the Princess of Wales's first name?' asked the interviewer.

'Sarah,' guessed the zombie wrongly.

'I'm afraid it's Diana,' said the interviewer.

'When he got outside, the zombie beckoned to his friend. 'They'll ask you the Princess of Wales's first name. I'll write it down and pin it to the lining of your jacket so that you don't forget.'

In went the second zombie. 'What is the Princess of Wales's first name?' asked the interviewer.

'Marks and Spencer,' said the zombie.

Why did the spook go to hospital?
To have his ghoul stones removed.

What should polite little monsters call their parents?
Dead and mummy.

A schoolboy's epitaph:
When I die, bury me deep,
Bury my history books at my feet.
Tell the teacher I've gone to rest,
and won't be back for my history test.

What did the skeleton say to his girlfriend?
    I love every bone in your body!

Smart Alec: When I'm feeling lonely I always
go to the graveyard.
Silly Billy: Why is that?
Smart Alec: There's always some body there.

*Why was the headless ghost sent to the mental
hospital?*
    Because he wasn't all there.

*Why do witches like to do their shopping in
markets rather than supermarkets?*
    Because they like to haggle.

How did the Egyptian ghost catch a cold?
  From its mummy.

What kind of girl does a mummy go out with?
  Any old girl he can dig up.

Igor: Dr Frankenstein, come quickly! You're
experiment's gone wrong and the ectoplasm is
breeding with the amoeba!
Dr Frankenstein: Don't bacilli!

Smart Alec: Excuse me asking such a personal
question, but what are those little bongo
things dangling from your ears?
Monster: They're just my eardrums.

Why did the monster have a tap on his head?
  Because he'd got water on the brain.

Witch: I've found a great way of keeping flies out of my kitchen.
Wizard: Tell me the secret.
Witch: You take a bucket, fill it with manure and put it in the middle of the sitting-room.

Monster Sleuth: I have a hunch!
Phantom Detective: I wouldn't say that – you're just a bit round-shouldered.

Witch: Is that the mail order department?
Manager: Yes it is.
Witch: I'd like a tall, dark, handsome green-eyed man, please, who can cook and clean and do the washing-up. And my friend would like a blond with blue eyes who can drive . . .

THERE'S THAT DOG. I'LL FRIGHTEN HIM WITH MY TEETH!

Zombie: That cannibal shouldn't be eating chips with his fingers, should he?
Werewolf: No, fingers should be eaten separately.

What do you call a fat monster who drowns in a river?
    A non-slimmer.

Spook: How big is a monster?
Phantom: What kind of monster?
Spook: A big one.
Phantom: How big?

What's the difference between an apple and a blue monster?
    An apple is red and green.

HAVE I GOT NEWS FOR HIM!

What's the name of the nervous spook who rides through the Egyptian desert?
  The Shake of Araby.

Did you hear about Dr Frankenstein's invention for cooking breakfast?
He crossed a chicken with an electric organ and now he's got Hammond eggs.

Ghost: And what are you going to do when you grow as big as your daddy?
Little Monster: Go on a diet.

What did the stupid ghost call his pet tiger?
  Spot.

Monster: You give me eerie ache!
Ghost: Sorry I spook!

What's a werewolf's favourite song?
  'A Pretty Ghoul is like a Malady.'

There once was a young spook called Pete,
Who never would play, work or eat.
He said, I don't care,
For Coke or eclair –
Can't you see that I'm dead on my feet?'

1st Witch: Every time it's misty I hear a
strange croaking noise coming from your
house.
2nd Witch: That would be my frog horn.

What's a skeleton?
  Bones with the person off.

What's Dracula's favourite society?
  The Consumer's Association.

What happens when the phantom cavalier loses his head?
  He sends for a head hunter.

Mummy, mummy, why do I keep going round in circles?
  If you don't shut up I'll nail your other foot to the floor.

What is a monster's last drink?
   His bier.

What did the werewolf eat after he'd had his teeth taken out?
   The dentist.

If Dracula knocked out a phantom-weight boxer, what would he be?
   Out for the Count.

Monster: I've got to walk 25 miles home.
Ghost: Why don't you take a train?
Monster: I did once, but my mother made me give it back.

1st Corpse: I didn't get a wink of sleep last night.
2nd Corpse: Day mares?
1st Corpse: No, two many flies.
2nd Corpse: Why didn't you dust them off?
1st Corpse: It was too dark for me to see if they needed dusting!

A man sat playing chess with a huge hairy purple monster in a pub. A stranger came in and sat down and in amazement watched them playing. When they'd finished the game he came over.

'I'm a movie producer,' he explained as he introduced himself. 'Your monster could make a fortune in Hollywood.'

The man just shrugged. 'He's not that clever,' he said dismissively. 'I've beaten him three times in the last four games.'

What do CND ghosts hold?
    Demon-stations.

Smart Alec: Do you want a game of vampires?
Silly Billy: For money?
Smart Alec: Yes, for very high stakes.

What happened when the werewolf met the five-headed monster?
   It was love at first fright.

Werewolf: Did you go to the party last night?
Ghost: Yes, it was great – we had a wail of a time.

Werewolf: Who was that lady I saw you with last night?
Cannibal: That wasn't a lady, that was my dinner.

What do you call a skeleton who goes out in the snow and rain without a coat or an umbrella?
   A numbskull.

FUME!

Little Cannibal: Look, look, I can juggle three heads at a time!
Cannibal Father: Stop playing with your food!

What did one witch's broom say to the other witch's broom?
    Have you heard the latest bit of dirt?

1st Witch: I've just brewed a cauldron of perfume.
2nd Witch: What are you going to call it?
1st Witch: 'High Heaven'
2nd Witch: It certainly stinks to it!
1st Witch: Shut up; it's a best-smeller.

A silly young fellow named Wide,
In a funeral procession was spied;
When asked, 'Who is dead?'
he giggled and said:
'See that coffin? It's the person inside!'

Who is the unluckiest monster?
The Luck Less Monster.

1st Witch: Why is your toad going dit-dit-da,
da-dit-da-dit?
2nd Witch: He'd a morse toad.

What are ghosts favourite trees?
  Ceme-trees.

What was the undertaker's motto?
  Never Say Die.

Titles from the Spooky Library:
Ghostly Voices by Mona Lott
The Spook in the Dungeon by Howey Wails
The Lady Vanishes by Peter Out
Japanese Phantoms by Hari Kari
The Spook from the Bottom of the Sea by
Constant Dripping.

Did you hear about the stupid monster who
had a piece of string hanging outside his
window? 'What's that for?' asked his friend.
    'It's my way of predicting the weather,'
explained the monster. 'When it swings about
I know it's windy, and when it's wet I know
it's raining.'

*Why does the Hound of the Baskervilles turn
round and round before he lies down for the
night?*
    Because he's a watchdog and he has to wind
    himself up.

When do monsters paint their toenails red?
    When they want to hide upside-down in
    your strawberry jam.

Why do monsters have flat feet?
   From jumping off wardrobes onto their
   victims.

A monster went to the doctor with a branch
growing out of his head. 'Hmm,' said the
doctor. 'I've no idea what it is.' The next
week the branch was covered in leaves and
blossom. 'I'm stumped,' said the doctor, 'but
you can try taking these pills.'
   When the monster came back a month later
the branch had grown into a tree, and just a
few weeks later he developed a small pond,
surrounded by trees and bushes, all of them
on the top of his head.
   'Ah!' said the doctor, 'I know what it is.
You've got a beauty spot!'

What's red and stupid?
   A blood clot.

Ghoul: You're little ghoul's grown!
Mrs Ghoul: Yes, she's certainly gruesome.

Where do elves go when they're feeling ill?
    The National Elf Service.

What kind of piano music do witches like best?
    Hagtime.

Spook: Did you hear about the exhausted jumping monster?
Witch: No – what about him?
Spook: He was out of bounds.

Why did the ghost look in the mirror?
    To see if he wasn't still there.

Did you hear about the spook who went on
the F-Plan diet?
He had beans on ghost twice a day.

1st Ghost: Shall I sit in this chair?
2nd Ghost: No, sit over there. This chair's for
rigor mortis-to sit in.

*What happened to the girl who slept with her
head under the pillow?*
   The fairies took her teeth out.

1st Ghost: It's so hot!
2nd Ghost: Would you like a drink?
1st Ghost: Oh yes – an ice ghoul one would be
lovely.

What do you get if you cross a zombie with a boy scout?
A creature that scares old ladies across the road.

Did you hear about the snooker-mad monster? He went to the doctor because he didn't feel well. 'What do you eat?' asked the doctor.
'For breakfast I have a couple of red snooker balls, and at lunchtime I grab a black, a pink and two yellows. I have a brown with my tea in the afternoon and then a blue and another pink for dinner.'
'I know why you're not feeling well,' exclaimed the doctor. 'You're not getting enough greens.'

Igor: I wish you'd do something about your table manners!
Frankenstein's Monster: Why, what's wrong with them?
Igor: You just bolt your food down.

What should you call three ghosts in a belfry?
Dead ringers.

Dr Frankenstein: I've just crossed a hyena with a snake.
Igor: What did you get?
Dr Frankenstein: I'm not sure, but if it starts to laugh I think we'd better join in.

A monster walked into the council rent office with a £5 note stuck in one ear and a £10 note in the other. You see, he was £15 in arrears.

Young Fred is gone, too soon alas!
He tried to trace escaping gas.
With lighted match he braves the fates –
Which blew him to the Pearly Gates.

How did the little monsters keep their teacher on her toes?
   They put drawing pins on her chair.

What do ghosts like in their coffee?
   Evaporated milk.

How do you stop a monster smelling?
  Cut off its nose.

Willie had a taste for gore,
So nailed his sister to the door.
His mother said, with humour quaint.
'Now, Willie, don't you scratch that paint!'

What has webbed feet, feathers, fangs and goes quack-quack?
  Count Duckula.

1st Cannibal: I really don't know what to make of my husband!
2nd Cannibal: How about a curry?

Which skeleton fought at the Battle of Waterloo?
   Napoleon Boney-parte.

How do you make a monster shrink?
   Give him condensed milk.

Doctor, doctor, I feel as if I'm at death's door!
   Don't worry, I'll pull you through.

Mummy, mummy, are you sure that this is the way the Italians make spaghetti bolognese?
   Shut up and get back in the saucepan.

1st Witch: You'll have to control your little boy better. He just bit me on the ankle.
Vampire Mother: That's only because he's not big enough to bite you on the neck.

Silly Billy: What kind of monster is that?
Smart Alec: A police monster, of course.
Silly Billy: It doesn't look much like a police monster to me.
Smart Alec: Well it wouldn't – it's in plain clothes.

Newsflash:
Two monsters have escaped from prison today. One is orange and 9ft tall and the other is green and yellow and 2ft 6in tall. The police are searching high and low for them.

Dracula: What kind of books do you like best?
Undertaker: Oh, anything with a grave plot.

ARREST THE SECOND JOKE FROM THE TOP

Dr Frankenstein: For my latest experiment I'm going to cross a rat with a woodpecker.
Igor: And what do you expect to get?
Dr Frankenstein: A rat-a-tat-tat.

Why was Dr Frankenstein's robot monster so silly?
Because he had a screw loose.

What do you call a monster who is married and has sixteen children?
Daddy.

Countess Dracula: Say something soft and sweet to me!
Dracula: Marshmallows, chocolate fudge cake . . .

A man found himself staying alone in a gloomy farmhouse out on the moors one wet and windy night. He went to bed and turned out the light, but a strange tapping noise stopped him from dropping off to sleep. Rap-rap-rap it went, and even though he put his pillow over his head he could still hear it. Furiously he got out of bed and went onto the landing. Rap-rap-rap . . . He could hear it coming from downstairs, so down he went, and into the gloomy kitchen. Rap-rap-rap. He followed the noise and discovered that it was coming from the cellar so, determined to put a stop to it, he lit a candle and ventured down the damp and creepy steps. Now the noise was louder, and the thing, whatever it was, was rapping harder. By the light of his flickering candle the man inspected the cellar. there was no one there, and nothing to make the noise. His fingers shook with fear, but he knew that he must go on and discover the source of the noise.

In one corner of the cellar was a pile of old rugs, and it was from there that the rapping noise seemed to be coming, louder and louder now. With his heart in his mouth he pulled the rugs apart and found a wooden box. Rap-rap-rap went the noise. Something, or *someone*, was in the box.

Terrified, he stood there for a moment. What could it be? A dismembered hand? A ghost trapped in the box for hundreds of years? Sweat trickled down his brow as he stood and wondered what to do. But there was nothing for it. Whatever hideous or evil thing was inside the box, he *had* to know. Slowly he eased open the creaking lid and peered inside. And there, at the bottom, and rapping away was – a sheet of wrapping paper . . .

Where does Supermonster shop for all the things he needs to keep him big and healthy and strong?

At a supermarket.

How can you tell the difference between a monster and a banana?

Try picking it up. If you can't, it's either a monster or a giant banana.

Epitaph:
Deep beneath this pile of stones
Lies all that's left of Billy Jones.
His name was Smith, it was not Jones,
But Smith, alas, don't rhyme with stones.

Monster: Dr Frankenstein is so funny!
Smart Alec: Is he?
Monster: He keeps *me* in stitches.

What should you do if you find a green monster in the garden?
 Wait until it ripens.

What should you call a witch who sits on the beach but is too scared to go into the sea?
 A chicken sandwitch.

Igor: Dr Frankenstein's been called in to help the England cricket team.
Monster: How's he going to do that?
Igor: He's going to cross a round black hat and a Ferrari to make a very fast bowler.

What did Frankenstein do when he split his sides laughing?
 He ran around until he had a stitch again.

What was the space monster's favourite game?
 He liked to play astronauts and crosses with real astronauts.

1st Dragon: I'm divorcing my husband for smoking in bed.
2nd Dragon: That doesn't sound a serious reason for divorce.
1st Dragon: He doesn't smoke cigarettes – he just smokes.

How do you make a slow monster fast?
   Don't feed him for a fortnight.

Dr Frankenstein: Help! Help!
Igor: What's wrong?
Dr Frankenstein: I crossed a lion with a parrot and it just bit my arm off.

Smart Alec: Is that a Scotch monster over there?
Spook: Yes – how did you know?
Smart Alec: Every time I get near him he tries to give me a nip.

What should you keep in a cellar?
   Whines and spirits.

What time is it when a monster sits on your car?
    Time to get a new car.

Witch: Eat up your greens, Frankenstein. They'll put colour into your cheeks.
Frankenstein's Monster: But I don't want green cheeks.

Little Monster: I've got a new hobby.
Little Ghost: What is it?
Little Monster: Worm collecting.
Little Ghost: That's unusual. What do you do once you've collected them?
Little Monster: Press them.

What game do little cannibals like to play at parties?
    Swallow my leader.
And what game do little ghosts play at parties?
    Haunt the thimble.

1st Monster: Did you hear that Humpty Dumpty fell off the wall?
2nd Monster: Yes – and they couldn't put him back together again.
1st Monster: Well, he never was all he was cracked up to be.

Silly Billy: What's the difference between a monster that's asleep and a monster that's awake?
Smart Alec: With some monsters it's difficult to tell.

Would you say that horror movies are spooktacular?

Ghost: Do you believe in the hereafter?
Phantom: Of course I do!
Ghost: Well, hereafter leave me alone!

TROUBLE IS –
NOW EVERYONE'S
GOT FALSE FANGS!

What did the dragon say when he saw St George in his shining armour?
   Oh no, not more tinned food.

Monster: My wife's cooking is awful! Last night she even managed to burn the salad.
Wizard: My wife's even worse. She can burn the washing-up water!

What did the zombie call his coffin?
   His snuff box.

What did E.T.'s mother say to him when he got home?
   Where on Earth have you been?

Dr Frankenstein: In my latest experiment I have crossed a jeep with a sheep dog.
Igor: And what did you get?
Dr Frankenstein: A land rover.

Did you hear about the monster who tried to join the Lonely Hearts Club?
He sent them his picture, but they sent it back with a note saying that no one else was *that* lonely.

What do male ghosts do standing up, lady monsters do sitting down, and werewolves do on three legs?
Shake hands.

Why are vampires artistic?
They're good at drawing blood.

Silly Billy: Do monsters like children?
Smart Alec: Yes, but they prefer roast beef and gravy.

Here lies a chap who met his fate
Because he put on too much weight.
To over-eating he was prone,
But now he's gained his final stone.

Who do ghosts call in if they don't feel well?
    The surgical spirit.

Why do witches ride broomsticks?
    So that they can sweep across the sky.

Witch: What happened to my pet frog?
Traffic Warden: He was parked on a double
yellow line, so I had him toad away.

1st Ghost: I'm very worried about my baby.
2nd Ghost: Why, does he keep crying?
1st Ghost: No, he's in such good spirits it's
quite unnatural.

A young ghost who hailed from Bengal,
Was asked to a fancy dress ball.
He decided to risk it
And went as a biscuit,
But a ghoul ate him up in the hall.

A farmer went to the market in a distant town
and had to spend the night in the local hotel
when it began to snow heavily. It seemed
rather a nice hotel and he liked his room.
There was only one thing that bothered him,
and that was a big green push-button by the
door. He puzzled about it for some time as he
got ready for bed, but he didn't like to push it.
Perhaps it was an alarm bell that would bring
the staff? Perhaps it was to call room service?
He went to bed still worrying about it, and all
night long he tossed and turned, wondering
what would happen if he touched it. Perhaps,
he wondered as he lay staring at the ceiling,
the hotel was haunted and this was a special
button to press in such an emergency. By the
time the sun rose the next morning he was in
such a state that he could bear it no longer
and crept across the room to where the bell
shone on the wall. Gathering all his courage,
he pressed his finger down firmly on the
button – and the central light came on.

1st Monster: You have to be really brave to string tennis raquets!
2nd Monster: Why?
1st Monster: It takes guts . . .

Who went into the werewolf's den and came out alive?
   The werewolf.

1st Monster: I'm going to France for my holidays.
2nd Monster: How are you going to cross the Channel?
1st Monster: I've got ferries at the bottom of my garden.

What do Catholic cannibals eat on Fridays?
   Fish and chaps.

Did you hear about Mrs Spellbinder's new twins?
   It's difficult to tell witch from witch.

Why did the monster have indigestion?
　He'd eaten someone who disagreed with him.

Why are monsters' fingers never more than eleven inches long?
　Because if they were twelve inches they'd be a foot.

What do ghosts pour on their roast beef?
　Gravey.

Monster: Doctor, I think I've got food poisoning!
Doctor: Have you eaten anything strange or unusual recently?
Monster: Yes, I ate a knight in armour yesterday.
Doctor: And did he smell all right when you took his armour off?
Monster: You mean I was supposed to take him out of the armour before I ate him?

Why did the little monster push her father into the deep freeze?
　Because she wanted frozen pop.

1st Monster: I'm getting married tomorrow, so shall we go out tonight for a drink?
2nd Monster: Yes, let's go and paint the town dead.

What should spooks wear in the rain?
  Boo-ts and ghoul-oshes.

What should you do with a blue monster?
  Tell him a joke and cheer him up.

What should you do when an abominable snowman sneezes?
  Run for cover.

Who is the wobbly monster's favourite artist?
   Bottijelli.

1st Monster: I'm so thirsty my tongue's hanging out.
2nd Monster: Oh – I thought it was your tie!

What vegetables does a werewolf like to eat with his bones?
   Marrow.

1st Witch: I always wear wellington boots in the winter.
2nd Witch: Yes, and I like lace-ups for spring.
1st Witch: And then for summer there are always open-toad sandals.

Can a toothless vampire bite you?
No, but he can give you a nasty suck.

What did the cannibal chief do when his daughter reached marriageable age?
He looked around for an edible bachelor.

1st Ghost: You can tell I'm getting old – I'm supposed to be invisible but I'm beginning to show.
2nd Ghost: I've got just the thing for you, vanishing cream.

Who speaks at the ghosts' press conferences?
The spooksperson.

What song do they sing at the Monster Cinema when the film finishes?
Ghoul Brittania.

Monster: Please, help me, doctor. You see, I prefer jeans to tracksuit trousers!
Doctor: That's not a problem. As a matter of fact *I* prefer jeans to tracksuit bottoms too.
Monster: What an incredible relief! And how do you like yours, doctor – roasted or grilled?

*What did Frankenstein's monster say when he
was struck by lightning?*

Thanks, I needed that.

Epitaph
The bomb went off too soon, alas,
And there John's story ceases.
The bits they found are buried here,
And so he rests in pieces.

Which little monster eats faster than any other?
   The goblin.

Which monster makes strange noises in its throat?
   A gargoyle.

What should you do if you find yourself surrounded by Dracula, Frankenstein, a zombie and a wild werewolf?
   Hope you're at a fancy dress party.

Smart Alec: Can you name four types of bird that can't fly?
Silly Billy: Ostriches, penguins, kiwis . . .
Smart Alec: And dead ones.